MALCOLM
Thank you for ... next
on

TAKE THE
NEXT
STEP

THE STORY OF *Guitar Aid*

Dave Sumner

DAVE SUMNER

O&U
Onwards & Upwards

Onwards and Upwards Publishers

4 The Old Smithy
London Road
Rockbeare
EX5 2EA
United Kingdom
www.onwardsandupwards.org

First edition, published in the United Kingdom by Onwards and Upwards Publishers Ltd. (2024).

ISBN: 978-1-78815-954-8
Typeface: Sabon LT

"

It's not for you to know the end, or yet to see the path, but to see the next step and take it.

Take the Next Step

Contents

I don't think there is a right or a wrong way of worshipping God. But music is a wonderful, fulfilling and emotional way to do so.

Through Guitar Aid many of you, young and old, have discovered the thrill of worship through music, so strum on, play on.

Sir Cliff Richard
Patron of Guitar Aid

Take the Next Step

About the Author

Dave Sumner is the founder and director of the Guitar Aid charity, which has given over 4,000 guitars across the globe, enabling worshippers to praise God with quality instruments. Dave felt the call of God to missions on his first trip to Romania in 1990, and there the vision of Guitar Aid was born. Dave loves to encourage others and is passionate about missions and worship. This passion has taken him to many nations around the world. His stories and clear vision will inspire you to 'take the next step' that God has for you. Dave lives in Exeter with his wife Liz and the family.

Guitar Aid contact details

Address	Dave Sumner
	Guitar Aid
	94 Gloucester Road
	Exeter
	EX4 2ED
Email	*guitaraid90@gmail.com*
Website	www.guitar-aid.com

Take the Next Step

I've long been an admirer of Dave's ministry, heart and determination. He's made it possible for me to put guitars into the hands of worship leaders across the world, from Mozambique to Mumbai. Having seen the power of music to change lives and draw people towards God, the importance of musical instruments for the kingdom can't be understated. I'm always blown away by Dave's faith, generosity and steadfast dedication to his mission. He is always looking for the next person to bless. This book is a powerful and inspiring insight into the man behind the ministry, and God's power to provide for those called according to his purposes! A great read.

Philippa Hanna

Take the Next Step

Foreword by Martin Smith

There are many books you can read on faith and mission.

Many books you can read on how to improve our lives, spiritually, physically and mentally.

But the thing that I love about this book is that it's 100% a real-life story of love, commitment, dedication and generosity.

It's the story about giving guitars away.

Gifting people with guitars doesn't necessarily grab the attention of the theologians or the big missionary organisations, but when you think about it, it's genius.

There are millions of people who live on this planet without access to fresh running water, enough food, clothing etc… so shouldn't feeding the poor be the priority of the church?

Why waste your life giving guitars away?

Well… here's the thing.

What is central to every community across the globe?

Music.

Dancing.

Singing together.

You get a community singing together and then the heavens open.

And when the heavens open, anything can happen.

What helps people sing? Guitars.

Guitar Aid has existed to provide people a musical instrument that will help them worship the creator of the universe.

And when a community worships a living God, all 'hell' breaks loose and miracles happen.

The rain falls, the rivers burst, the crops explode, bellies are nourished, disease is banished, kings and queens bow down, people prosper, wars cease and nations return to Christ.

So no, it's not just a guitar.

It's a 'weapon' of worship.

The shepherd boy David played his own harp to King Saul, filling the courts with the glory of God, so much so that the evil, tormenting spirit had to leave the king.

Just a guitar, eh?

I'm so proud of Dave and the team who have tirelessly and humbly dedicated their lives to this cause.

You will love this book. It will inspire you as it's inspired me.

Read it and then commit to sponsoring them if you can, and enjoy seeing the nations around the world lifting up a holy sound.

Martin Smith

For the last three decades, UK worship artist, songwriter and producer Martin Smith has been penning songs that bring fresh air to the lungs of the Church. From 'Did You Feel The Mountains Tremble?' and 'Waiting Here For You' to 'I Could Sing Of Your Love Forever' and 'History Maker', Martin's songs have connected generations and inspired and influenced worship leaders and worshippers alike. And whether as frontman for the groundbreaking band Delirious?, lead singer of Army Of Bones or as a solo worship leader, Martin has been involved with almost every aspect of the modern worship movement.

"The goal of mission is worship" – one day every tribe, tongue, language and people group will stand before the throne of God and worship (Revelation 7:9). Dave Sumner, with his God-given vision of Guitar Aid, helps achieve this goal. The heart that comes through in every chapter, as Dave shares stories of nations, historical events, miracles, friendships and adventure, is to re-source worshippers. Guitar Aid is a great mission ministry. I've known Dave now for the past five years, since becoming Mission Director of AOG GB. I have always been inspired by the ministry of Guitar Aid; after reading *Take The Next Step*, I respect him even more. As you read this book, allow faith to stir in your heart, allow God to show you your 'next step' in his mission.

Pastor Kirk McAtear
Missions Director, AOG GB

Take the Next Step

Preface

Having been on so many missions over the years, I have often been asked if we have written any of our mission's stories down. I have, but not until now have I attempted to put them all together. We invited Miro Toth, a well-known worship leader from Slovakia, to lead one of our Guitar Aid celebrations. After the event, on the journey back to the airport, he gave me this challenge: "Dave, you owe it to future generations to write down your missions stories and how Guitar Aid started." So from that time, I started to do what Miro had said.

The purpose of writing this is to encourage each and every Christian that God has a plan for your life. My mother often would recall a prophetic word, "It's not for us to know the end, or yet to see the path, but to see the next step and take it." Hence the title, *Take the Next Step*.

In the secular realm, we are often asked, "What is your five-year plan? Where do you see yourself five years from now?" I want to encourage you, wherever you are, God has a *next step* you can take. Our missions, and Guitar Aid in particular, have prospered by seeking the next step, seeing it and taking it.

I trust as you read this book, you will be inspired to trust God and let him show you that step.

Take the Next Step

My name is Jude Muchiri. I was born and raised in Mathare, the second largest slum in Kenya. It has a population of 900,000 people. 60% youth and children. Ever since the tender age of 14, I had a passion to reach out to the unchurched in the community. Before I got a guitar, I had a dream of doing worship music on the streets. I dreamt of a time when I could raise a new sound from the slums. A sound of hope that is full of life. This dream is now a reality, and I wouldn't want to continue without saying a big thank you for the ministry of Guitar Aid and what you are doing around the world. Your impact is bigger than you can imagine.

Jude
Mathare, Kenya

Take the Next Step

Introduction

Making a guitar for Paul McCartney

If you were to ask me how Guitar Aid began, I might reply that it all started when I made a guitar for Paul McCartney.

Yes, really – *the* Sir Paul McCartney!

When I was younger, I used to do puppet shows for Sunday School with a large puppet theatre that had been kindly made by Bill Hill. As part of the puppet show, the puppets would sing. We had the gospel Wombles! I made little model guitars for them to play. This got me into making small replica guitars. Paul Day, who is known as the guitar guru, lives near us and got to hear about my small guitar-making skills. He recommended me to the Performing Rights Society when they were looking for someone to make a replica Hofner Violin Bass to be presented to Sir Paul McCartney.

I will never forget the phone call. Brian Engle, a member of the New Seekers, rang me at work. He wanted to meet me as soon as possible.

I was sworn to secrecy, as they wanted the presentation to be a surprise. Brian came to Exeter by train, first class, every week to check progress. Each time he came he would be wearing ever-increasing amounts of gold. Brian brought down a full-size Hofner Violin Bass for me to take measurements from. It took me over two hours to record 250 dimensions to make sure what I produced would be exactly to scale. It took six weeks of hard work to make the trophy.

The social club at work had arranged a shopping trip to London, so we took the trophy with us in a carrier bag. I will never forget handing it over at the P.R.S. headquarters and them immediately locking it away in a safe! In November 1989, the P.R.S. celebrated their 75th anniversary by presenting Sir Paul McCartney with the model that I had made. This appeared on the front page of many national newspapers, including the *Daily Mail.* I also contacted our local paper, the *Express and Echo*, where my brother John worked, and they came and interviewed me and put a picture of me with the guitar on the front page on the same day.

I have a photo of the guitar at home signed by Sir Paul. It says:

To Dave, thanks mate, great work, Paul McCartney.

So I reckon I'm his mate!

"

Putting musical instruments into the hands of those who either couldn't find or afford them releases much praise and worship to God and brings heaven down to earth. I thoroughly commend the work of Dave Sumner and Guitar Aid for your support.

Bryn Haworth

Take the Next Step

1

Shaped to serve

Although it was a guitar made for Paul McCartney and a mission trip to Romania that directly led to the launch of Guitar Aid, to really understand the heart behind the charity, we need to go back further. God was shaping my life for what was to come already from a young age.

God's faithfulness in my early years

I was born and lived my first few years in Harrogate. My parents had moved there after getting married in order to follow my dad's calling into ministry, having originally met at Bristol Bible College. Dad worked for Hoover, but also became the pastor of a church.

Life was not easy for my parents in Harrogate. At one time, Dad was taken ill and was in hospital for many months. As Christmas approached, Mum had no way of getting us Christmas presents. Christmas Eve came and there was a knock on the door. A kind gentleman handed something to her. "The Lord told me to bring this to you," he said. It was a train set for us boys – how wonderful the provision of God is! So from a very early age we learned of God's faithfulness.

The pioneering missions spirit was part of family life. At Hoover, Dad met another Christian called David Richards, who invited him to Scotland. Mum and Dad both felt the call of God to move north, so when they heard from him, they left everything and moved to pioneer a church there.

Before leaving Harrogate, my brother John and I sat on the knees of the pastor who would take over from Dad. That pastor was David

Hathaway, the evangelist, founder and president of Eurovision Mission to Europe. I was three, John was five, and as little boys David sat us on his knees, spoke kindly to us and prayed for us. Is it any wonder we ended up being called to missions?

Childhood in Scotland – choosing to follow Jesus

I have fond memories of our time in Scotland, especially our home in Glenrothes. It was in the little church that Mum and Dad pioneered in Innerleven, Scotland, that I learned to love the missionary stories. We often had visiting speakers. The Manchester Trekkers were one of my favourites; then there was Uncle Francis and his talking doll, Colin Blackman and so many more – but the most significant was Teddy Hodgson. My brother John and I sat spellbound, listening to his stories of how God had led him to Africa. We loved Teddy Hodgson. In those days we didn't have a TV, so you can imagine the shock when our neighbours came to tell us that the news had covered a story of missionaries being martyred. We went next door at evening news time, only to hear that Teddy Hodgson and Elton Knauff had both been murdered in the Belgian Congo. To think Teddy had only been with us a few months before. What admiration we had for these men who were willing to sacrifice their lives for others. It was an honour to have men like this stay in our home.

At school, we learned nothing of English history, but listened attentively to the things that David Livingstone achieved in his life. These memories grounded us in the desire to take the love of Jesus to the furthest corners of the globe.

It was a missionary from Ceylon, now Sri Lanka, that had the biggest impact on our lives. He explained the way of salvation so simply and invited those who wanted to follow Jesus to raise their hands. John and I were in different parts of the meeting and, unknown to each other, we both responded. My desire to follow Jesus was so great that after the service I rushed up to Dad to see if I could do anything to help him; he duly let me pack away his briefcase. The decision to follow Jesus at the age of five for me and seven for John was the best decision of our lives. Through the many ups and downs of life, it is a decision we have never gone back on.

As children, one of the Scottish traditions we loved was a wedding. When the bride left her home for the wedding, the father of the bride threw money out of the window of the car. News soon got around where the weddings were on a Saturday. John and I loved to join in the scramble as the car left and the money flew out!

It was also in Scotland that we learned what it is to hear from God. One day, Mum took us to visit a lady that had been causing trouble. As we approached the house, John and I knew there would be difficulty. Mum knocked on the door and we waited, but no one answered. She then turned to us boys and said, "You see, all God wanted was my obedience." We learned a valuable lesson that day.

Teen years in Wales – learning generosity

In Scotland, Dad worked his paid job alongside pioneering the church, but when I was 13, the opportunity came for him to step into full-time ministry in Wales. So we moved again.

The youth group of Newbridge Pentecostal Church proved to be a great blessing to John and me.[1] We learned to grow spiritually there and loved the annual visits to the Assemblies of God general conference. We also both played electric guitars in the worship band. Saving up for gear was a high priority for us. I learned about generosity from John Palmer, who was an elder at the church at the time. He would ask us how we were doing, saving up for the next piece of equipment we needed. John would then put his hand in his pocket and give us money to help us get what we needed sooner. This meant so much to us as young people. John was investing in the kingdom; little did he know at that time that he was setting me on a journey on which generosity would be a hallmark.

As 'pastor's kids', we were expected to follow all the rules, but some of the rules were too inward-thinking. Richard Wurmbrand, the amazing pioneering Romanian evangelist, came to Newbridge – not to our church, but to Beulah Baptist Church. However, the oversight of our church would not cancel the midweek meeting to allow us to attend the Thursday evening event. My brother and I, like good pastor's kids, walked past the meeting being held by Richard Wurmbrand and went to our own service. I feel we missed out on an outstanding opportunity to hear from this great man of God. This experience was one of our first lessons in realising that God uses many denominations to build his

---

[1] John met his wife Dorcas in Wales; they have been happily married ever since, and have had two children, Andrew and Judith.

kingdom. Later on in life, we read how Richard had suffered for his faith, in his book *Tortured for Christ*. Oh, how we wished we had personally met him!

After five years in Newbridge, Dad was invited to be the pastor at one of two churches, either in Corby or in Exeter. I am delighted to say he chose Exeter.

Exeter, The Gospel Crusaders and Life Explosion

We moved to Exeter in 1972 and have lived happily here ever since. I love everything about Exeter; it is a truly wonderful place to live. It's where I met Liz, my wife, and we have four children: Chris, Ben, Dan and Becky. I now also have three wonderful grandchildren in Elias, Orla and Evan. Our home overlooks the city, and we can see the cathedral, the church spires, and the skyline going on for miles. In the early mornings, we see some glorious sunrises. Exeter is truly home – a place I will always love.

Ever since deciding to follow Jesus as a little boy, I had always had a deep desire to serve him. Service now took the form of being Sunday school superintendent of Exeter AOG[2], and also being part of The Gospel Crusaders, a Christian outreach band, with John, Dorcas and Peter Rooke. At our peak we were invited to play at the Assemblies of God general conference. We even managed to be part of the album they recorded that year, the theme of which was 'Maintaining the glow'.

My interest in worship led me on to five very happy years playing in the Christian rock band Life Explosion. It was during those years that I met, fell in love with and married Liz. The band helped me appreciate the many churches in Exeter, as each member of the band came from a different congregation: Anglican, Baptist, Brethren, Free Church and me, a Pentecostal. We had a particularly large Mercedes van that was converted. The front half had very luxurious seats, wall to wall carpets, a coffee machine and everything a touring rock band could wish for. The back half was sectioned off with a bulkhead, where we stored the equipment. Most weekends we would head off anywhere in the West Country – Bristol, Cornwall, you name it, we went there. We would take a couple of hours setting up and then give a gospel concert. It was such a joy to see young people make a decision for Christ at these events.

---

[2] Assemblies of God

Afterward, everything was packed up, and we headed home late into the evening.

I have fond memories of the times with Phil, John, Mac and Pin. The band's biggest gig was to play to a packed-out audience at Queen's Hall, Barnstaple as part of Mission England. We also made an album entitled 'Right Direction'.

At the time when the band was about to finish, I received an invitation from my friend Bill Hill to join him every other Tuesday to play the guitar and worship with the inmates at Exeter Prison. This service continued for 30 years. However, I avoid going around telling people that I spent 30 years serving in Exeter Prison – that could easily be badly misunderstood... In fact, later in life when I had a family, I was there one day with Bill when the phone rang at my home. My daughter answered, saying, "My dad's not here; he is in prison!" Liz and I had a good laugh about that! I was often also joined by Steve McDaniel, a brilliant guitarist with a great testimony of how God had delivered him from drug addiction.

Take the Next Step

"

Music deserves to be played by the young and the old, the rich and the poor. Guitar Aid is a truly rock and roll missionary response to letting people sing a new song all over the earth.

Martin Smith

Take the Next Step

2

What have you got in your hands?

That's the question God asked Moses. It is the same question he asked me before I went on my first mission trip to Romania in 1990. I looked down and I saw it was a guitar that I had in my hands.

"Anything else?"

"I can fix things," was my reply.

These two things were exactly what God wanted from me. Surrendering these things to the Lord was the start of Guitar Aid. I would never have believed where it would eventually lead. It's easy for us to miss God's plan for our lives by looking for something too spiritual. It's often the practical things that bring spiritual fruit – like Guitar Aid.

That which you have in your hands is the very thing God wants to use.

Exeter and my first insight into Eastern Europe

Although John and I had missed the Richard Wurmbrand meeting, we found out what was happening in Romania and Eastern Europe during the 1970s through a lovely lady called Shirley Clear. A remarkable example to us of faith and obedience, she would pack her bags and say, "Well, Lord, where do you want me to go?" Often she would end up in an obscure part of the world following God's lead. Shirley spoke to us passionately about the suffering in Romania.

I then became more aware of Communist countries on my honeymoon in Corfu. Liz and I invited our friends Dave and Pat from

York to our wedding, but they said they couldn't come as they were on holiday in Corfu. "That's strange!" we replied. "That's where we are going on honeymoon." So, we planned to meet up.

When they picked us up in a minibus, we were surprised to see a few more members of their church[3] on holiday with them. One of these was Keith Hall, the pastor's son. We were all going to a point on the island of Corfu that was closest to Albania. I knew nothing about Albania when I got on that minibus, but by the time we got to our destination, I felt like an expert on all things Albanian thanks to the enthusiasm of Keith. I found out it was a closed nation; no one was allowed in or out. I heard about the dictator, Enver Hoxha, and his declaration that Albania was the first atheistic county in the world. I heard how difficult it must be for Christians there. As we stood looking across the water to Albania, gunboats were patrolling, ready to shoot anyone who tried to get near the country and also willing to shoot anyone who dared to think about escaping. With the zoom lens on my camera I could clearly see the Communist-style blocks of flats. I wondered what life was like for those people. Why could we not go there? Why were we not free to visit them?

This was the first time I really became aware of the plight of Communist countries and the repression that it could bring. When I returned home, someone told me about the book *The Hitchhiker's Guide to Europe*. On the page about Albania were two words: "Forget it!"

John's first visit to Hungary

For John, his first contact with Eastern Europe was in 1986 with his family: Andrew aged four, Judith aged two and Dorcas his wife. Earlier in the year, they had seen a programme on TV called *Standing Up for Joe*, about a little boy receiving treatment at the Peto Institute in Budapest. John and Dorcas wrote a letter to the Peto Institute and were accepted for a month's treatment. Now Andrew would be able to receive the help he needed, having had complications at his birth.

The people were so kind and helpful to them, but the life was so different. They were greeted by soldiers with machine guns at the steps as they got off the plane. Police with guns were on every street corner. Many times they found themselves asking God the question, *what are we*

---

[3] Rock Church York

doing here, yet knowing that if they trusted the Lord, he would direct their paths.

Over the next two years, they went back three more times, spending a total of four and a half months in Hungary. There, John fell in love with Eastern Europe. Boarding the plane home after the final visit, he stopped on the steps to have a last look over Budapest and clearly heard God say to him, "You will be back." And true to his promise, God did later enable John to return.

Visiting Romania as Communism collapses

In 1989, the world was going through dramatic changes: the Berlin wall was coming down, and Romania was being liberated from years of dictatorship. Nicolae Ceausescu was executed by his own soldiers, and suddenly Eastern Europe was becoming open.

My brother John went on the first convoy to Romania that left the UK in January 1990. He came home a changed person and immediately started to plan a return trip. The trip John had been on was organised by INCARE, the humanitarian aid wing of Assemblies of God. John was able to go on this trip without having to think about the organisational side of it. Had he been in charge, they would have stayed much longer in Romania than they did. He came home determined to go back and to take others with him, so that they too could catch the vision. I'll pass you over to John to tell his story:

> "I watched at the end of 1989 as the Berlin wall came down and reports started to come out of Romania: thousands of orphaned children locked up 24 hours a day, many tied or chained to their cots, and some even chained to radiators. We heard first-hand accounts of tanks crushing people to death in Timisoara square. Remembering how the people in Hungary had helped us as a family, I could not sit back and do nothing. A few days later, a letter arrived at our church asking us to help fill two lorries with aid from the South West, to be driven to Romania the fourth week of January 1990, along with nine lorries from different parts of the country.

> "I set about fundraising as much as I possibly could. I phoned the organisers and offered to help drive one of the lorries, but was told that it was only pastors who would be allowed to drive. My

head could not take this in, so every other day I phoned asking to drive, until eventually I was told not to phone again – 'This trip is for pastors only.' I continued to collect and fundraise, my bags packed, my passport on top and I was ready to go. Four days before the convoy was due to depart, I received a frantic phone call from the convoy organisers: was I still willing to drive to Romania at such short notice, as one of the pastors had dropped out? My answer? 'Try to stop me!' Strange how God makes a way when man says there is none.

"*We set off from Exeter, meeting the other lorries at Dover. There were 33 of us, 11 vehicles. It took three days to get to Romania, including up to four hours stuck at every border along the way. In Hungary, the lorry I was driving blew a back tyre. We looked underneath for the spare, only to realise there was not one there. Of all the vehicles, ours was the only one with double wheels at the back, so we gingerly carried on, eventually arriving at the Romanian border around midnight. Everything was black, with the odd light here and there.*

"*We were treated like heroes. Once through the border, we headed for our contacts in Arad, whom we met at the big church, Bujak. There were many tears and hugs, and friendships were made that have lasted a lifetime. They had prepared a meal for us of chicken soup, the chicken head hanging out of one bowl, the feet out of another. They stood around to watch us eat. It is an experience I will never forget, as they gave us all they had.*

"*The next morning, we started to unload, but it was becoming impossible because the children were totally surrounding the vehicles. I had taken my guitar with me, so I had the idea to get it and sing some children's songs; it was not long before I had over 100 children around me, and unloading went without a hitch.*

"*The decision was made to leave at midday, so we went for a walk along a muddy, potholed road and I vowed to God that I would return as soon as was possible. We were in the country a total of 18 hours – 18 hours that changed my life.*"

"You can't eat a guitar."

When John came back from his first trip to Romania, he immediately started to organise a return trip. I was the first to volunteer to come along. We also found that Okehampton AOG were keen to come along and provide their own lorry. As mentioned in the Introduction, John worked for the local newspaper, the *Express and Echo*. He had managed to get a lot of publicity when he was raising funds for his son Andrew to go to Hungary, so he was in an ideal position to fundraise and publicise what was eventually to become 'Aid to Eastern Europe'. John contacted Maddern Transport and paid the deposit for two lorries. We soon mobilised a workforce to start collecting food, clothing, toys, toiletries and all the things that they needed in Romania. It didn't take long for us to completely fill the two lorries.

In preparation for this trip, God had asked me the question about what I had in my hands. I understood that he wanted me to use guitars and fixing them as a way to serve him, so I planned to take six guitars with me to Romania to give away.

"But you can't eat a guitar," someone protested when they heard my plan.

"You can't play a tin of beans," was my quick retort.

In fact, at the time I had no idea of the impact that giving away guitars would have.

We set off as Romanian Relief Convoy in March 1990. This was before mobile phones had taken off, so in each cab was a CB radio. This proved to be an invaluable way of keeping in touch as we headed off for Romania. We made it to Aachen, Germany, the first night. In the morning, John realised the logistical nightmare of trying to get nine drivers ready and off to go as soon as possible. We drove on and ended the next day in Austria, after which it took another day to get to Budapest, where repairs were needed on the Okehampton lorry. We finally made it to Romania on the fourth day – three overnight stops! That was never going to happen again; John would make sure of that. Subsequent trips were much more disciplined and refined. Mark Wade, who is now a missionary living in Romania, was on that first trip with us.

On the first night of arrival at Arad, Romania, we were greeted by the Ardeu family, and Aurel was the first person I met as we entered the church. That evening, we took our guitars out and spontaneously sang worship songs, much to the delight of our newfound friends in Romania. *This was the very moment I felt the call of God on my life for missions.* Since then, there has been no looking back.

Giving the first guitar

On the last Sunday we were in Arad, I had been singing and playing a Washburn guitar. After the service, the youth pastor asked me if he could play it for a while. With great excitement, the young people gathered round him and they sang a song in Romanian.

When he came to hand the guitar back to me, I said, "No, you keep it; it's a gift!"

His response was incredible: "I don't believe it! *My own guitar!*"

He held it above his head as if he had won a major sporting trophy. That vivid image has remained firmly with me: looking down a poorly lit street with the cold winter chill in the air, seeing in the distance a young man waving a guitar above his head.

This moment changed my life and something was born inside me. I now had a passion to give guitars to those who needed them but couldn't afford them.

So it was really on a cold winter's night in March 1990 that Guitar Aid was born.

"

Guitar Aid is a fresh, exciting initiative,
which deserves much recognition. It's
good to see such a practical response
to an obvious need.

Matt Redman

Take the Next Step

3

Guitar Aid takes off

I had made the golden guitar for Paul McCartney just before the trip to Romania. Now, upon returning home, I found that all the music magazines were featuring articles about it. Seeing an opportunity, I contacted every guitar importer in the country.

"I'm the guy who made the guitar for Paul McCartney," I said. "I've just come back from Romania and I want to take guitars to them. Can I buy any of your damaged guitars, or have you any guitars you would donate?"

I was able to make contact with all the top people in the guitar business. God used the Paul McCartney guitar to open this massive door.

John Hornby Skewes were the first company to help me; Fender also said they would help. The relationship with JHS & Co has continued to this day. We have literally bought thousands of guitars from them to be given for worship across the globe.

I chatted with my parents about my fresh vision and they were very enthusiastic. My dad gave me a gift and said, "Open an account in the name of Guitar Aid." So I did, and it has continued to this day.

Others catch the vision

Planning for the next trip to Romania got underway as soon as we returned home from the first one. Word had got around the local churches of what had been achieved there. Isca fellowship wanted to come on a trip, as did St Thomas Baptist church, so the era of taking lorries across Europe to Romania began, and continued for the next five years.

We hired our lorries from Maddern Transport in Exeter, and after the second time of going to Romania, we started to have an impact on the owners of the company. At the family Christmas get-together, Maurice Heaver, the Director of Maddern, announced to the family, "Next year we are going to Romania to help the orphans there." So the next trip, we had a 7.5-ton lorry, Isca had a 7.5-ton lorry and Maddern Transport provided a massive 21-ton lorry! They paid all the fuel and accommodation costs for the three drivers. This was such an encouragement to us. We had no problem filling all three lorries, such was the support and interest that the Romanian orphanage situation had created. Many of our trips comprised of three lorries travelling with up to nine guys across Europe.

In those days, crossing a border was a nightmare. Each country had different levels of bureaucracy. We knew that the aid we were taking was vital to the lives of those who would receive it. We saw things in Romania that had an enormous impact on our lives. Once when I visited the hospital in Arad, a pickup truck arrived with a man screaming in the back. We watched them carry him into the hospital – an awful sight in itself, but nothing compared to seeing someone run back to the truck to pick up his legs that had been severed by a tram. These images stayed with us for months.

Secret police and the most polluted place on earth

On the early trips, we were not always aware of the dangers. One time, we thought it would be great to see where the battles took place. Cassius, our Romanian friend, offered to take us to the place where the secret police operated from. We thought this was a great idea until they invited us in to see the vantage point they had over the city. As we went in, the heavy steel door slammed behind us! Suddenly it didn't seem such a good idea. They took us to the top floor, where the whole wall had been blown out. Sure enough, through that hole, they had a magnificent view of the city. Much to our relief, they then took us downstairs and let us out. "Never again!" was our response to that experience.

The sight of children in Copsa Mica, a town in Romania, is something we cannot forget. They greeted us, semi-naked and black from head to toe with the soot that belched out of the Communist factory. Nearby, the trees were black; everything you looked at was black, due to the continual pollution from the factory. The conditions in the factory were so bad that they recruited workers from the prison. Copsa Mica had a strong evil presence which left you feeling slimed as you left. *National Geographic* magazine had a feature saying that Copsa Mica was the most polluted place on earth. Blocks of flats lay derelict there, so we asked why this was. We were told that the workers from the factory got drunk as soon as they were paid, and they had burned down their own flats in a drunken rage. There were three blocks of flats that had been burned, leaving them as an adventure playground for kids. It's quite a sight to see children as young as eight on the roof of a five-storey block of flats, leaning perilously over the edge. As parents, we could hardly believe what we were seeing. "Do not open the door of your car; do not get out," were our instructions as we drove past this sight. The children looked like wild animals; the adults didn't look much better. We left with heavy hearts, determined to do whatever we could to help this desperate place.

Friends in Romania

We drove on to Medias to visit a bookshop that my brother had read about in a Christian magazine. We arrived on a day that Jenny and Gusthi, the missionaries that were there, had run out of food. They decided to pray until the food came. When we knocked on the door, the reception we received was unforgettable. They were able to stock up from what we had on the lorries. This was the start of a great friendship, as we would visit them many more times in the future.

We made many friends in Romania. One was Ted Bora, who was one of our interpreters. On one occasion, we went to the big Pentecostal church in Arad. They had a visiting preacher from USA, and Ted was given the job of interpreting for him. The preacher told the congregation that they needed to suffer and they replied with an amen. He then told them they would be persecuted and they again said amen. Finally, he told them they would have to learn to pray all through the night; still they said amen. We were very confused by this point. We knew for sure that the Romanian church had suffered, been persecuted and had learned to pray. We asked Ted after the meeting, how did you get such a response from the difficult things that the American was saying to them? Ted answered, "You see, he preached his sermon, I preached mine!"

We went to Romania to give to those in need. We made many friends and soon realised that they would do anything for us. One of the young people that had a guitar from us asked, "Is there anything *we* can get *you*?" I said that I would love to have a flag from the revolution, one that had a hole cut in it from where the Communist emblem used to be. A few hours later, he returned with a flag. "I give it to you in Jesus' name." Little did we know that he had climbed the flagpole of the football stadium to get us our prized trophy!

What started as just one flag...

When I go to a country for the first time, I am usually asked that same question: Is there anything you want? My reply is now always that I would love to have a full-size flag. So now, after John and I have visited over 50 countries, I have a really good selection of flags, as you can imagine. These flags are on display at the Guitar Aid room at Riverside Church in Exeter and in the Guitar Aid office. Each flag I have brought back has a story to tell.

I did miss getting a flag one time in Bosnia. We went to Tuzla and met up with a pastor. As is our custom, we offered to take him out for lunch. He must have thought that we were well off, so he took us to a top class hotel. We were thrilled with the stories he told of how God had helped them during the war in the former Yugoslavia. We were told that overnight the banks were closed and everything went to the war effort. It was so hard in those times; for example, one member of his church exchanged a Volkswagen Golf car for a sack of potatoes, some eggs and a chicken. Many during this time went hungry and feared for their lives. After the stories and the meal came the bill, and some bill it was! We had received silver service and were now going to pay for it! Later that day, walking around Tuzla, I spotted a Bosnian flag. As John held all the foreign currency, I asked him if we could buy the flag. His response was classic: "I'm afraid, Dave, that you have eaten the flag at that posh restaurant!" I knew exactly what he meant; we just didn't have enough of the local currency left. From that day on, we always asked our hosts to take us to a simple place to eat and always checked it would not be beyond our budget.

New Year trip to Lipova

We had just returned from Romania in the November, and such was the interest in helping this needy country that the warehouse was still full of goods. I felt that the need was so great that it demanded a response. We decided that just after Christmas we would set off for Romania again. My brother had already been there four times and had now completely run out of holidays, so he couldn't go. This gave me the opportunity to lead my first mission.

We told our contact in Romania that we wanted to visit a village as well as the city of Arad. Previous to leaving, I had been looking at a map with my father-in-law and he had pointed to Lipova saying, "I wonder what's there?" You can imagine our surprise then, when our contact decided to take us to that very village. The highlight of that trip was to arrive at the state orphanage in Lipova, to find that they had run out of food. What a blessing to be there at such a needy time and take in box after box of precious supplies. We made a video of that visit and filmed two little brothers, Andre and Alex. Three years later, these same two brothers went to the Haven of Hope Orphanage in Lipova.

Working and serving

John and I never let full time secular employment stop us from going on missions. In fact, both our firms were very supportive of our involvement in Romania and Eastern Europe. However, my workplace, Howmet, soon realised that going on missions, or 'aid trips' as they saw it, was my passion. The managers called me to see them and, along with HR, agreed to let me work overtime as 'make up time' and bank it towards time off for missions. Most years, I would work an extra 80 hours in this way, enabling me to have an extra two weeks' holiday that was used exclusively for missions. Whenever I went to Romania, the personnel manager would call me into the office and usually give £500 towards the cost of fuel for the trips.

I found favour with successive managers in Howmet. Jack Bodner, who was very high up in the global organisation, told me that I had inspired him to take up playing guitar. He said he loved what Guitar Aid was doing. Support and encouragement were given from both work colleagues and the unions.

God had not led us along the path of full-time ministry, but in many cases, being from a working background gave us favour with the many pastors in poorer countries that had to combine working with serving due to financial constraints. We encourage people to follow the call of God on their lives, even when the job you have doesn't seem perfect.

Austria extended stay

The guys we hired lorries from were getting quite used to our regular visits to Romania. One time, they gave us a lorry they had just bought, but the clutch gave out halfway across Germany. We towed this one with one of the other trucks. Then the clutch on this second one finally gave out on the Austrian/Hungarian border. So we were stuck! We had only one vehicle working out of three. We stayed put for three days while they drove out with two replacement gear boxes. With snow on the ground and temperatures of minus fifteen, we managed, by some sort of divine intervention, to get under the trucks and change the gear boxes. The sheer weight of that unit took every ounce of strength we had, but again, we did not let this setback stop us. We continued on to have another great mission.

Mookie the dog

When we drove across Romania, we had three lorries and three men per lorry, which meant there would be nine of us to feed. We have had a few experiences of tasting food we didn't like and quickly learned what to say no to.

For example, one time we stopped off for lunch, where something was quickly prepared for us – rather *too* quickly. That evening, all nine of us took it in turns to use the only toilet available; the queue seemed to last all night!

On another occasion, we had a BBQ at Dr Julia's in Gales. We made it clear to the drivers that they should only eat well-cooked meat. Anything we didn't like the look of, we sneakily gave to Mookie the dog. None of us suffered any bad consequences from that meal. However, the next time we visited Dr Julia, we asked about Mookie, as he didn't seem to be about. "Oh, Mookie, poor Mookie... He died three days after your last visit." It made us realise how unwell we would have been if we had eaten the undercooked food.

I am very glad to tell you a few words about Dave Sumner and his team, who are doing a great service for musicians from all over the churches. I remember clearly the moment when, almost 10 years ago, I got my first electric guitar. Being just a child, I could not afford it, but through Guitar Aid, God sent me a gift. The blessing didn't stop there, but through many years God blessed me and the entire worship team with other musical instruments through Dave and his team. Guitar Aid is a great blessing for us, and I hope and pray to God to bless them for their efforts and what they are doing.

Sergei
Lipova, Romania

Take the Next Step

4

Albania

The places where John and I worked were near each other. At lunchtime we would often meet and chat about missions. One day we said, "Imagine being able to fly somewhere and not having to drive 3,000 miles!" This sounded like a dream. But that weekend Roy David, the late father of our good friend Andy David, was speaking at our church. I was really moved by what he said.

I rang him later that day and said, "Any time you need guitars for missions, I will be glad to help you."

While we were on the phone, he asked me, "Are you interested in going to Albania, as a group of pastors are going and they could do with a couple of musicians?" He also mentioned my brother John could come too.

What an opportunity!

We found out there was a team of seven of us going from the UK. We decided that was an opportunity to take seven guitars. When we arrived at the airport, all the pastors wondered what we were doing. But all the guitars were taken and very much needed in Albania.

On the plane journey I had the latest edition of National Geographic magazine. In it was an article, 'Albania Opens Its Door'. Wow, here we were actually going at the very first opportunity!.

"Who do you say I am?"

We arrived in Tirana and drove to Pogradec. We could hardly believe that God had opened the door for this opportunity. I didn't realise how much fun and joking would go on when a group of pastors were let loose on a mission.

On the flight over, one of them asked the steward, "What do you think we are?"

Her reply was classic: "A rugby team…"

"No, we are ministers!"

We arrived in Pogradec to be met by Arnold Geiger, a missionary from Germany with Nehemiah Organisation. The plan for the week was to hold evangelical meetings in the football stadium.

Our first night was quite eventful. The place we were staying at was also the venue for an Albanian wedding. They had a band with electric guitars plugged in and ready to go. My brother and I asked if they would like a song in English. They loved it; we sang 'Amazing Grace'.

At breakfast the following morning, some of the pastors said, "Did you hear that last night? Amazing grace…"

"Yes, that was us!" we replied.

Albania's first baptism in half a century

Having just opened up, Albania was completely wild. At nighttime, it was normal to have your sleep disturbed by gun shots. When we got to the stadium for the first meeting, it was incredible to look out and see the football stand full of people eager to hear what we had to say.

I will never forget worshipping in that stadium, with Mike Bettany on keyboard, my brother and me on guitar, and also on guitar was a very young Miro Toth from Slovakia. We sang, "Shine, Jesus, shine, fill *this land* with the Father's glory." What a moment – to feel God's presence so powerfully in front of hundreds hungry for God.

We had open-air meetings from an open back truck, visited hospitals, schools and villages. At the end of the week, we held what was to be the first baptismal service for over 50 years in that nation. I will never forget the day when Andy and the other young people proclaimed their love for Jesus as we baptised them.

Of all the people on that trip, George Ridley was the one who immediately caught the vision for Albania. He said, "The need is great, the opportunity is there. If not now, then when? If not us, then who?" John and I decided this was for us, so we contacted George and said we would love to go with him when he returned to Albania.

Building relationships

On that first trip to Albania, we made sure we took full advantage of the diversity of countries represented. Wieslaw Ziemba was there from Poland; we became good friends with him. There was Lubo who lived in Czech Republic and Miro Toth from Slovakia. Our friendship and relationship started in Albania and it didn't stop there. On several occasions we have been in the homes of Wieslaw, Lubo and Miro. We have preached in their churches and taken many guitars to them. We made so many long-term connections on that first Albania trip.

Wherever we go, it is our intention to build strong, long-term friendships. This principle has been one of the foundations our missions have been built on.

Lightforce International

George Ridley, the director of Lightforce International, did not hesitate in asking us to join him as he planned meeting up with government officials in Albania. So, a few months after the first visit, the three of us set off. In Albania, we met up with Mr Palushi, deputy prime minister.

George said he wanted to work somewhere where no one else was working. He showed us the Lure region, so the plan was set for us to go there. On the journey, we were accompanied by armed guards. This seemed a bit strange until we were overtaken by a blacked-out mafia car. Our guards told us that once they had seen the guns, they decided to leave us alone. It might have been a completely different story had they not been with us.

We arrived at the Lure to be confronted by outstanding scenery alongside the most dilapidated buildings we had ever seen. For sure this place needed help big time. We stayed in a house where we sat on mats on the second floor. The lower floor was for the animals. Evidently, the heat from them helped keep the house warm. They told us we were the first Western people to stay in the village for over 50 years. What a privilege! In the morning, they showed us the hospital. George decided this would be an excellent project for Lightforce International.

On the way home, we asked him, "Is there anything we can do to help?"

He quickly replied, "Get me a Land Rover."

Angels unawares?

On our second visit to Albania, with George Ridley, we made plans to work in the Lure region with Deputy Prime Minister Palushi. That evening, George wanted to rest, whereas my brother and I were keen to see as much as we could.

We caught the bus into the centre of Tirana, and after looking around for a few hours, we decided to head back. Not sure which bus to catch, we thought the walk would do us good, so we headed back in the direction we had come from. However, it seemed a lot further than we had remembered and very soon it started to get dark. We walked along a lonely stretch next to a field, looking very conspicuous – my brother John with his briefcase and me carrying the ever-present full-size VHS video camera with BBC stickers, just to give access to those difficult places.

We were alone when suddenly a car sped past us and screeched to a halt. Simultaneously, all four doors opened; they had guns! Our lives suddenly flashed before our eyes, and we realised how stupid we had been.

We cried out to God to help us. Then, seemingly from nowhere, two soldiers appeared. It was hard to see where they had come from. We looked at them in surprise.

Some words, like 'Coca Cola', are universally understood. 'Taxi' is such a word. "Taxi, taxi?" we asked the soldiers.

They pointed back to the city and said, "Ah, taxi."

They were wearing camouflage uniforms with a small Italian flag. We walked with them for about half an hour and eventually got to Scanderbeg square in the centre of Tirana. They pointed to the Hotel Tirana in the corner and said, "Taxi."

We then turned round to thank them, but there was no one there. The vast area around us was deserted.

I believe God sent angels to protect us at a time of extreme danger.

"We need your Land Rover; we don't need you."

On a previous trip, a pastor had told us about his business of buying and selling caravans. John and I thought it sounded quite easy. We knew God had a plan for us to work together, and perhaps this was it. So we bought our first caravan, sold it for a profit and bought another one. After a few sales, we ended up buying a lame duck; we lost money on that one.

We now thought about George's request. We had this fund available from the caravan project, so when George had asked us to buy him a Land Rover, we immediately knew where the money would come from. Now we spoke to our friendly Land Rover dealers and told them the plan. They were quite impressed with the project and our enthusiasm to help out. They came up with the perfect vehicle: a 110 Land Rover, white with a big roof-rack. Perfect!

This vehicle became our pride and joy. We spent months preparing it for the mission. The plan was that it would ferry people to and from Albania for a six-month period. We were to be on the first mission to take it there. We arrived at the centre to meet up with the others going on the trip and to show our new missions vehicle.

We soon realised there were more people on the team than would fit in the vehicle. We were told, "We need your Land Rover; we don't need you." So John and I returned home with our tails between our legs and licked our wounds.

We were still happy for our vehicle to be used, so the plan was that sometime during the six months of service, we would go out to Albania to see the project and see how it was being used. But after half a year, George returned the Land Rover.

We spent more time fixing everything that it needed, so that George could have it the next year for another six months' service.

New and old working together

After the disappointment of not driving out with our Land Rover to Albania, the next best thing was to fly out to meet up with the Land Rover. By this time, George had purchased his own Land Rover for Lightforce. What a joy to see the two vehicles side by side, ferrying teams of young people from the UK to Albania.

The transformation that was taking place in the hospital in the lure was incredible. John and I were both compelled to don a pair of overalls and get stuck in to painting and helping renovate alongside the Lightforce team.

During our time there, a team drove out from Milton Keynes. They arrived exhausted, having had very little sleep on the way. George ran a tight budget and made sure every penny possible went on the project in the Lure. The comfort of the team was secondary to this. We met some wonderful people on this visit; Gesina Blaue, a Dutch lady, was fully committed to the people of Albania. She became a good friend of ours.

When that period of our Land Rover's use finished, George thanked us and said he wouldn't need it again. When we got it home, we realised that we now had our own missions vehicle. So we made plans to take it to Romania. No longer was there a need to hire a lorry and then take it back after the mission.

The missing camera

We were fortunate that my brother John worked at the local newspaper, so whenever we went on missions, you could count on them to publish some sort of feature. On one occasion, John had a call from the general manager to go to his office. He was keen to find out exactly what John would be doing and what would be achieved. It was the time when we were heavily involved in renovating a hospital in the northern, mountainous region of Albania. The boss said that if John took pictures of the trip, then he would pay all his expenses and cover the story on his return.

Just as we were about to set off for the hospital, something went wrong with John's camera. Gesina Blaue, the director of one of the charities we were working with, said we could borrow hers instead. We had plenty of opportunities to take photos as we worked on that hospital alongside a team of people from the UK, and we stayed there a few days. But at one point, John put Gesina's camera down for a brief moment to wash his hands and when he looked round, it was gone...

What a disaster! How could he face Gesina? How could he face his boss?

To say John was despondent is an understatement; he felt like the man in the Bible who had lost the axe head: "Alas, Lord, it was borrowed..."

So John said aloud to God, "Either you are with me or you are not. If I get the camera back, I will know you are with me. If not, I will know that going on missions is not what you want me to do."

That got me praying as hard as John.

When the time to leave came, we all piled into the Land Rover, John with a heavy heart. As we pulled away, the engine stalled, and it took an hour to get it going again. Twice more this happened. We had been due to leave at 6am; it was now 8.30. Then, as we finally pulled away, in the distance we could see a group of people running towards us. The man at the front had something dangling from his neck.

John shouted, "Stop! They are bringing the camera back."

Sure enough, they ran up to the Land Rover and handed John the camera.

As we drove away, we heard the leader of the group mutter, "John and his blessed camera… We should have left at 6am…"

Anything stolen in Albania, in normal circumstances, is never returned. Thank God for the extraordinary!

Ralf's Fender guitar

On one of our many visits to Albania, we were in Tirana, where the pastor of the International Church said we must meet Ralf, his worship leader. Ralf was in the most successful Albanian band when he became a Christian. Black Iceberg, Ralf's band, were on TV and playing at mass open-air concerts. Pastor Rodney was concerned that this lifestyle could compromise his faith.

Ralf said, "With the band, I will have girls, money, fame and guitars. In the church, I don't even have my own guitar.

Rodney replied, "What type of guitar would you like?"

Ralf said, "A Fender."

"Let's pray," said Rodney.

Three days later, we arrived to meet up with Ralf. I said, "I have a guitar for you," and handed him a Fender.

We became great friends with Ralf. One time we were there, he led the March for Jesus rally with over 3,000 people, using one of our guitars. Ralf travelled extensively with us in our Land Rover, the length and breadth of Albania.

Adventures in Italy

In one period, I had many requests for guitars from Albania – 17 letters in total. We realised that God was speaking through these letters. I looked at my stock of guitars and took every one we could. We loaded up 86 instruments and set off on the long journey, travelling the full length of Italy and catching the ferry from Bari to Durres.

We got as far as Milan and started looking for somewhere to stop for the night. Eventually, feeling very tired, we found a paved area that looked ideal. We settled down in the back of the Land Rover to get some rest. Then the next morning we woke to the sound of heavy traffic, only to realise we had parked in the middle of a roundabout!

The only problem we encountered on the trip was with the Italian customs. They just were not happy with the fact that we had so many guitars on board, and they refused to let us get on the ferry. We told them we were musicians and wanted to teach the children in Albania to play the guitar, but still they said no. The customs officials then demanded that we open a couple of the boxes with guitars in.

"Play!" they shouted at us.

John and I looked at each other and wondered what songs they would know. One of our group said, "The Beatles," so we started to sing a few bars of 'She loves you'.

To our amazement, the two border guards joined in, singing and laughing like a couple of kids! Suddenly, there was no problem and we were allowed to go straight on the ferry.

Ongoing trips to Albania

This was an amazing time for Albania's new churches. Every town and city was experiencing growth and new Christians on a weekly basis. We were privileged to sow into this great time of spiritual harvest. Ralf helped us make sure the guitars went exactly where they were needed most.

On the return ferry, we met a young Albanian who was excited about getting his new motorbike from Italy.

"What type of bike are you getting?" we asked him.

"Whatever they steal!" was his reply.

That's how it was in those days!

We continued to visit Albania many times and learned to love the people and the country. Ralf spent time teaching us the exact pronunciation of 'I exalt thee' in Albanian. To this day, I remember that song with affection. I can still remember all the words in Albanian!

Albanian village ministry

Life was very primitive in the Albanian villages. One time, the Jesus film was to be shown in a remote village. In order to watch the film, they tapped into the overhead electric cables for the power. Someone climbed up the electricity pylon and hooked the two wires on the appropriate lines. The dangerous nature of this practice was further reinforced when we saw a teenager with one arm. We were told he had lost his other arm in an electrical mishap.

We visited a pastor, Stephen, who had been called to work for the Lord in a remote village in Albania. We were thanking God for our Land Rover as we approached the village. The only way through was to drive through a stream that came halfway up the vehicle. The journey this far had been on very bumpy, hilly tracks, which would have been difficult for an ordinary vehicle to navigate.

When we arrived, we asked the pastor how had he been accepted as a Westerner by the locals in the village. He explained that when he arrived with his family, they asked him if he trusted them; he responded that he did. They then presented him with a very difficult dilemma.

"If you trust us, then you will give us your son to take to our home for the weekend; then we will bring him back. If you agree, we will trust you."

Wow, what a difficult position! It's so easy to say that you trust them, but when faced with this kind of challenge, it's not easy. After a lot of heart-searching with his wife, they finally agreed to it.

He told us, "Watching my nine-year-old son disappear over the hill with a family that I didn't know was one of the hardest things I have done in my life."

That weekend, Stephen and his wife didn't sleep. They spent the whole time praying their son would be safe.

"The relief of seeing our son come back over the hill on the Monday was absolutely incredible!"

From that time onwards, they had the total respect of the villagers and were able to start a church there. What a testimony!

Stephen had a nice Guild acoustic guitar, made in the USA. I noticed it had a lot of bad dents on the front of the guitar and asked him how it had happened. He had lent the guitar to an Albanian to play, and for every time he strummed the guitar, he would hit the front of the guitar with his plectrum. This created a *strum, thump, strum, thump* kind of rhythm. Wonderful though it may have sounded, each thump was putting a deep mark on the front of the guitar!

While we were there, Stephen asked his son to do something and his son replied, "Aww… Dad" – like most young people; sometimes they don't want to do something you have asked them.

His dad replied, "Servant heart, son, servant heart."

His son got up immediately and did what his dad had asked him to do.

Now, when faced with a difficult challenge or being asked to do something I am not keen to do, "Servant heart" often comes to my mind.

Since I met Dave and John Sumner, some years ago in Albania, I have been so much impressed every time with their love of Christ and the great joy they have in serving him. The simple testimonies of the miraculous work of God in their lives and the unique ministry they are doing faithfully brings great encouragement to Christians they visit. Providing guitars to those in need is a very visible help, but also shows that the real Christian ministry is not limited to full-time people and to our way of thinking about ministry. This ministry is an example of God's invention. I believe God wants to call more people to unique ministry in his kingdom.

Pastor Wieslaw Ziemba
Legnica, Poland

Take the Next Step

5

Armenia

One Christmas, I received a newsletter from Sam Yegnesar of Love Armenia, a charity based in the UK. Something about it made me want to go to Armenia. John and I decided to make contact with Sam, so we arranged to meet at their headquarters in Surrey. We instantly connected with him and asked, "Is there anything we can do to help?" He thought that our ministry of promoting praise and worship would be greatly appreciated in the country. So the date was set, the plan was made and we set off with three big boxes of guitars and a lot of faith that the airline would accept them.

Not a traditional postal service

The week before our visit to Armenia, our friend Shirley Clear was there. She was due to fly home on the same day we would fly out. Hers was a morning flight, ours an afternoon flight.

While in Armenia, Shirley met a lady who had a children's work in the north of the country with over 200 children. The lady could play guitar but didn't have one. The question was, how could Shirley let us know?

She wrote a letter when she landed in Paris, and went to the information desk and told them, "Later today, two brothers are going to come to the desk and ask for directions to the Yerevan gate. When they do, give them this letter."

A few hours later, we did a thing we never usually do. We seemed to be confused as to where our gate was, so we went to the information desk to ask directions. The response was, "Ah! You must be the two brothers. I have a letter for you from a lady in England."

Suffice to say, the young lady in Armenia got her guitar.

Shirley would often take a guitar on our behalf on her missions. The most memorable time was in Alaska. As she gave a guitar to a pastor there, he held it to his chest. As he did, Shirley saw tears rolling down his face, dripping on to the front of the guitar. This is a moment she will always cherish. It makes us realise how much the guitars are appreciated. Only Shirley could arrange to get a letter to us halfway to Armenia!

Soviet-style travel

Our first shock on this mission was when we realised that we would be travelling on the old Russian airline, Aeroflot. When I got to my seat on the plane, I noticed that my seatbelt didn't have any buckle, and I had to tie it 'Indiana Jones style' and just accept that was the way it was. At the front of the plane, a very large Russian was standing, arms folded, scrutinising everyone's move, especially ours. The cracked glass on the window and intimidating atmosphere did nothing to make us feel at ease.

As we took off, the plane lurched into the air as if under a heavy burden. Just then, all the overhead lockers popped open under the strain, raining down their contents on unsuspecting travellers below.

This kind of travel was a new experience for us and an introduction to Soviet-style Communist living.

We arrived without a problem, and our three boxes of guitars were shipped as if they were nothing unusual. We were told to look out for someone with a 'Love Armenia' sign. As soon as we saw it, we recognised the person holding it: Romic, an IBTI[4] student we had met on one of our visits to see John Wildrian at Burgess Hill. Romic was the only person we knew in the whole of Armenia, and he comes to pick us up! This was going to be exciting.

Actually, exciting was an understatement. They packed us into a van with no seats, so we sat on wooden stools next to our boxes of guitars. We felt every bump on the road, and we swished from side to side as we turned each corner. Armenia was a place of so much tension.

Interrogated by 'the brothers'

We woke the next morning to the magnificent sight of Mount Ararat; although in Turkey, it is very close to Yerevan. We were with a weary

---

[4] International Bible Training Institute

people that had suffered much, but this had done nothing to hinder their faith. Being new, we were summoned to meet with 'the brothers'. This was quite an experience! The brothers were a group made up of the church leaders. They wanted to know who we were, what we believed and what we intended to do in their country. It was clear they wanted to establish our credentials before allowing us on to their pulpits and into their churches

'The room' of the brothers did not seem to us to be a friendly place. "Are you charismatic or are you Pentecostal?" was the first question they fired at us. Our answer of "charismatic Pentecostals" seemed to completely floor them. But after a few more questions they seemed to warm to us, which came as a relief both to us and to Romic who was with us.

What we soon became aware of was, this was a war zone, with conflict in Nagorna-Karabakh, only 80 miles away. Perhaps the speed at which they drove us around reflected the fear of being taken by the snatch squads that operated each night to relieve the soldiers on the front line. The night we arrived, our host Pastor Nodar had to leave us quickly as one of his congregation had been arrested. Nodar had to try to get him out of prison after being snatched on the street, ready to be taken for war duty. Fortunately, Nodar was successful in his task.

Secret meetings in the woods

Everything we did in Armenia was done with the fear that the authorities might not like it. Our first meeting was in a massive theatre where the only bits of equipment were a generator, a P.A system, a keyboard and one electric light. I was asked to sing, so with my heart thumping, I stood in front of about 1,500 people. I sang from my heart in English, 'This is my desire'. This must have sounded very foreign to them. In the darkness, I could see an old lady weeping. Yerevan was tragic, yet also an amazing blessing. The dimly lit room added to the whole atmosphere. People were groaning and crying as they prayed. The presence of God was tangible in that place. We were so privileged to be there, sharing in the difficult life they live, witnessing such an outpouring of prayer.

The next day, we were to have an open air meeting. This was an open air like no other. We got into a car and sped off. We ended up in the middle of some woods. From all directions, cars turned up. If our meeting were seen by the secret police, we would be in trouble and, as Westerners, probably end up in prison. The same P.A. system, generator and keyboard arrived with a faithful crew that would set it up. In these circumstances, they really know how to worship. They sang with passion and a feeling of desperation. To hear their harmonies made you want to weep; it seemed like they were pouring out their heart and soul with every note. What a time we had, meeting with what seemed to be the underground church. This gave us a glimpse of how persecuted Christians have to operate in countries that do not accept the gospel.

Each night, as we went back to our small, meagre apartment, our sleep was interrupted by gunshots. The next day, the dead dogs lying on the side of the road answered our question as to what had been going on. Evidently, this happens on a weekly basis to try to rid the city of stray dogs. Our time in Armenia is one I could never forget.

There had been an earthquake in the northern part of Armenia a few years earlier, but nothing had been rebuilt, and if anything, it was getting worse. People lived in large, round metal containers. They had rigged electricity inside them direct from overhead cables. Inside the container were two bare wires; the switch was two more bare wires that you hooked on. The people had lived in these containers for so long that numbers were painted on the outside so that they could locate their home.

The last evening we were in Armenia was a Tuesday night. They put on a special meeting for us and, incredibly, about 600 people turned up. This was to be a special and humbling time for us as we shared the platform with Bishop Haik's son. Bishop Haik was martyred for his faith in Iran; this had only recently happened. To be with his son at this time really reinforced to us the cost some have to pay for sharing their faith. For sure, we were spending time with the persecuted church.

We think we have enough fuel

We boarded a plane home via Paris, but we seemed to be sitting on the tarmac for a long time. The sun was blazing down, and the plane was getting hotter and hotter. Among some of the passengers, tempers were starting to rise, so the attendants decided to give us the inflight meal while we were on the ground. Eventually, after three hours, we finally took off. As we levelled off, the pilot broadcast the message, "Sorry for the delay, but we don't have enough fuel to get to Paris. We have arranged to stop off in Bulgaria to purchase some more fuel, as we think we have enough fuel to get us there." We were learning to pray without ceasing, while others were just panicking!

As we took off, we sat next to a nuclear scientist from France. He pointed out the nuclear reactor to us. "It's the same as the one in Chernobyl," he told us. Not good for an area prone to earthquakes!

We spent much of the time on this trip feeling quite hungry, as the level of poverty there was quite extreme; food seemed so scarce. We finally arrived in Paris. No Burger King 'Whopper' I have ever had has tasted as good as the one I had there! What a contrast to where we had just been! We came home with a spirit of appreciation for many of the things in life that we take for granted at home in the UK.

One song that reminds me of this mission is, 'I lift my eyes up, to the mountains, where does my help come from?' Mount Ararat is an awesome sight!

Take the Next Step

"

So excited to partner with Guitar Aid.
My dad bought me my first guitar and
it changed my life. It meant I could
write songs that have connected with
many people. It's so wonderful to be
able to present that opportunity to
someone else – someone who otherwise would be unable to afford an
instrument. Guitar Aid is a beautiful
ministry!

Philippa Hanna
Singer, songwriter and author

Take the Next Step

6

Romania

In 1991, we were shown a piece of land in Lipova, Romania, where they had a vision to build a church and an orphanage. They bought the land and started the work of converting the existing buildings into a functioning orphanage. The next year, about the same time our Land Rover was given back to us, we received a letter from Pastor Otniel Luca in Romania. I received one and John received one. We had said to each other that we wouldn't go back to Romania until someone invited us. Well, here was the invite...

The five stages of missions

There are five stages of missions, and responses to what you are doing on missions: appreciation, anticipation, expectation, entitlement and dependency. The first three are quite natural responses, but a spirit of entitlement and subsequent dependency are both things to be avoided.

After the first mission trip to Albania, John and I had hired the lorries just one last time to return to Romania. Having seen the poverty in Albania and the need there, we were now in a better position to compare where our help was most needed. When we arrived in Romania in October 1992, nearly three years after freedom had come to the nation, we were greeted by some people who immediately asked what we had on the lorry – almost before they even welcomed us! This reaction forced us to consider our mission there. TV and Western culture had arrived. No longer did we all get together to sing after a service; we all went to our separate homes. This made us think that for the time being, we would focus on Albania and see how things developed in Romania.

John and I chatted about the change of culture that had taken place and decided that, for now, we wouldn't return until someone invited us and showed that we were indeed needed. It seemed a spirit of entitlement had come to some of the people we were working with there. We started to think about all the countries around Romania: Ukraine, Serbia, Croatia, Bosnia, the list goes on. John and I had both become more aware that missions involved so much more than giving humanitarian aid. It was about the call to follow the command of Jesus: to go into all the world.

Now, however, we had received a specific invitation through the letters sent to us, which told us that they were opening an orphanage in Lipova called the Haven of Hope. Would we be willing to help them with this project?

Return to Romania

We got in touch with George Ridley, who had used our Land Rover for the past two years, and asked him if we could borrow a trailer from him. He agreed, so the plan was set to take aid to the orphanage, not in a hired lorry but in our own missions vehicle.

We had a great system for driving the lorries. We had a team of three who would alternate roles; we would drive, then navigate and then rest. This worked perfectly in two-hour stints. But who would the third person for this trip be? John suggested Terry Harris. I agreed, so John phoned Terry with a call that would change his life.

Terry had just retired. He had felt God tell him it was time to sell his Porsche and that God was going to start a new chapter in his life. Now, Terry could hardly believe what John was saying, but he didn't hesitate to reply with a yes. Terry is a skilled mechanic and took delight in servicing and looking after the mechanical side of the Land Rover. We now had our team.

What a delight to travel across Europe in our own vehicle, knowing we would not need to give it back after the trip. During our drive, we often said to each other, "I wonder how many others will be there when we arrive?"

We eventually arrived at the Romanian border, where we were met by Otty. Otniel Luca, or Otty as we knew him, was the pastor of the Pentecostal church and the original founder of the orphanage. Our first question was, "How many others are here?"

We were so surprised by his reply: "No one. I only sent two invitations; one to John and one to you." How glad we were that we had answered the call.

Otty said, "As I was praying who to send for, God spoke to me to ask John and Dave, so I did."

What a blessing to be at the very start of the Haven of Hope Orphanage in Lipova, Romania.

Over the garden fence

Sometimes, what starts out as a perfectly normal conversation can have far-reaching consequences. At the bottom of our garden, we had a Christian family that had heard about our visits to Romania. The mother of the family spoke to me over the garden fence.

"Our daughter Gemma would love to go to Romania."

I had all the contacts and proceeded to find out what options were available to Gemma. It was arranged that she would go over to Romania for a week to see how she liked it and see if there was anything she could do to help. She came home, having felt the call of God on her life to be a missionary there. As a result of this chance conversation, Gemma ended up living in Romania and being one of the key people running the Haven of Hope Orphanage in Lipova.

Gemma told how she learned the language. "I was in America nannying for three months, with a plan to save money and return to the UK for university, but I felt God was calling me back to Romania. My argument to God was that I found communication really hard, as I couldn't speak Romanian. From then on I dreamt each night, remembering conversations around me in Romanian. When I returned to Romania, I was able to speak enough to communicate well. Another six months and I was fluent."

Gemma lived at the orphanage from September 1997 to April 2009. There were many times that Gemma got us through the borders due to her local knowledge and understanding of the procedures. On numerous occasions, we had to get in touch with her as we were having problems with customs officials. Usually the problem would be solved with $10 inside the passport. This might not seem right to us, but Gemma assured us, in Romania it was the only way. Each time we visited, it was like a breath of fresh air, having someone from our hometown in the orphanage.

Publicity leads to gifts

Many of the guitar magazines were happy to feature the work of Guitar Aid. As a result of this, Neil Murray from Whitesnake got to hear about our work. He came to Exeter with Peter Green, Cozy Powell and a few others.

When I asked at the Forte Hotel reception for Neil Murray, they looked at me rather strangely. They called his room and immediately he said, "Oh yeah, I'll be right down to see him." He gave me two guitars, one of which was in a case with 'Whitesnake' painted on the side. He said I could do what I wanted with them, even sell them to buy more guitars, so I did. With the money from these two guitars, I was able to buy a batch of 48. It's great to have the respect of the people in the music business who have a desire to give something back to help those less fortunate than themselves. One time someone gave me a Gibson, Les Paul, which raised money for many guitars.

'My Story' – Westcountry Television

Word seemed to have got around about what Guitar Aid was doing. One day I received a phone call from Westcountry Television to say they would like to feature the work of Guitar Aid on the *My Story* programme. It was such a pleasure to share how it was developing. The camera crew spent a whole day filming with me, and the end result was a series of five-minute programmes that came on twice a day, just before the Westcountry News. The programme featured my family, my work, church and all aspects of the work of Guitar Aid. Those programmes can still be viewed on the Guitar Aid website.

I must admit, I have a little chuckle at how young I look in these programmes; it was quite a long time ago now! They say everyone has 15 minutes of fame – well, this was my turn! People came up to me saying that they had seen me on TV talking about Guitar Aid. The way the programmes were presented and edited was nothing short of exceptional.

"

Our beginnings [at Joshua Church] were not easy as we lacked instruments. We prayed that God would send people to help us. One of these was brother David Sumner from Guitar Aid. They have helped for so many years, the churches and musicians. The quality of the worship sound improved with every guitar we received. May God bless the Guitar Aid team and bring prosperity, so they can continue to give, blessing others with better sounds, better instruments and better guitars.

Sebastian Lela
Worship Leader, Joshua Church
Deva, Romania

Take the Next Step

7

1,000 pounds and 1,000 guitars

One day, we sat with Pastor Bohuslav Wojnar, enjoying a meal together in his home town in Czech Republic – on one of our many visits there. The town is split in half by a river – one half in Czechia, the other in Poland. You only have to cross that river to see different cars, different food and a different language spoken. The meal was to celebrate giving our 1,000th guitar.

We reminded Bohuslav that the first time we had met them, they were meeting in a hotel; now they had a magnificent church building facing a massive area of Communist-style tower blocks. Bohuslav told us an interesting story about the first time a McDonald's had come to Prague. He said that as he entered the place, tears filled his eyes as he realised the West had finally arrived. Having been active in Eastern Europe since 1990, we can understand why this experience meant so much to him.

During that visit to the Czech Republic, I noticed that the church had a large glass pot on the edge of the platform, which people put their prayer requests in. Just a few weeks before the trip, someone had given me a gift of £1,000 to buy guitars that I needed. I placed a note in the pot, praying that this gift would be the first fruit of a new outpouring of finance for the work of Guitar Aid. This ended up being the case, with many more gifts about to come in, and a new step forward for Guitar Aid.

Guitar Aid branded instruments

As we started to approach the 1,000th guitar mark, I was at the stage where I was getting rather tired of repairing guitars. I told the Lord that I couldn't face many more.

I knew they made guitars in Romania, as many of the damaged ones from John Hornby Skewes had 'Romania' on the label. I noticed over the years that the quality was improving and, due to exchange rates, the price was going down. Whenever we visited Romania, I used to check out the guitars at the Scala department store in Arad. So in November 2000, I bought three of these instruments with the idea of turning them into electro acoustic guitars.

On a wedding anniversary trip to Prague, we stayed in the Bible College as we were not able to afford to stay in a hotel. Each evening we would walk down to the centre of Prague from the Bible College. One time we went to the centre of a square, where they were getting people to sponsor a brick in an orphanage. "Sign this bit of paper and you will be providing a brick towards the project." Many people were signing up.

The whole idea of sponsorship hit me. If only we could have our own guitars made, brand new, people might sponsor them. I wasted no time in contacting JHS to see if it was possible to pursue the idea of our own instruments.

At first, the answer was no; then one Sunday morning, just after a brilliant meeting in Nairobi, Kenya, I was talking to Bishop Simon Githigi. He asked me how my mobile phone worked and he wanted to try it, so he phoned my wife, Liz. He was so excited to talk to someone in the UK. But Liz had something equally exciting to tell me; she told me that I had received a letter from JHS to say they were willing to make the guitars: a quantity of 100 at £39 each!

The possibility of sponsorship was born. I placed the order for the first 100 Guitar Aid branded electro acoustic guitars in red, blue and green.

A big surprise for the church

We had the first Guitar Aid celebration night at Riverside Church in Exeter, my home church. There I shared the vision of having our own brand guitars. But unknown to everyone there, we had something waiting in hiding. At the appropriate moment, we pulled a curtain down to reveal the 100 ready guitars! People were so surprised to realise that we had taken this big step.

A businessman at our church asked, "How much do these guitars cost?"

"£39 each," I replied.

He said, "I'd like to sponsor some," and in a Manchester accent he added something that shocked me: "N'undred!"

I soon realised he wanted to sponsor *100 guitars*! I could hardly believe it.

He said, "Show me the receipt for these guitars and I will buy the next hundred."

God had honoured our step of faith, and Guitar Aid was entering a new level of giving. The concept of being able to sponsor a guitar for £39 made it both affordable and gave specific involvement to those who wanted to support the work.

Meeting the director of the Hora factory

During the next few years, we established contact with the Hora factory in Reghin. We visited them five times, each time trying to introduce new ideas and develop both the quality and style of guitars made in Romania. One consignment of 100 guitars had the controls upside down, and the shape of the cutaway ranged from acceptable to awful! Tolerances, templates and minimum standards had to be established. It was like stepping back to the Communist era visiting the factory. The offices still had a picture of Nicolae Ceausescu on the wall.

Since then, we have continued to have our own brand instruments made. The quality of these instruments has steadily improved over the years. We regularly order these quality guitars, with the lead time from order to delivery sometimes taking many months due to the complexity of production in China.

Phone card era

In the early days, it was difficult to make ends meet. I would buy a batch of a dozen guitars and then, after repairing them, I would sell a couple to pay for the next batch of guitars. As well as strings, people needed plectrums. I found the thickness of a phone card was perfect to be used as a plectrum. As a toolmaker, I found it relatively easy to make a press tool to stamp out perfectly shaped plectrums. That led me to get my hands on as many phone cards as possible.

I found that Exeter University had its own Mercury card in both £2 and £10 units. I started to collect the cards myself and soon found out that not only were the phone cards good for plectrums but also that collectors were willing to buy cards off me. For about a two year period, when phone card collecting was popular, about 25% of my income for Guitar Aid came from selling phone cards.

A collector and producer of phone cards, Pellenor Promotions, contacted me and decided to have a set of limited edition phone cards made, with the proceeds going to our trips to Romania. This raised £3,000 for us and also gave Romanian Relief Convoy a permanent listing in the Stanley Gibbons Phone Card catalogue.

The idea of using phone cards as plectrums was entered into a competition with British Telecom. They wanted to find the best use of a used phone card – and guess what? It won!

Eddie's watch

I inherited a watch from Eddie, my next-door neighbour. I didn't really know what it was worth, so I put it in a drawer. Five years later, we were clearing out that drawer and I looked again at that watch. I found a shop that sold them and went to get a new battery and strap so I could use it.

My hearing has never been that good, and I thought the sales assistant had said a battery would be £16, which I thought was a bit expensive for a battery! I asked her if she had a spare strap. She replied, "Yes, £150." I must have looked shocked. "This is a very expensive watch," she explained.

Just then I saw the till register £60 for the battery.

"I thought it was £16," I said, and I decided not to have the job done.

As I walked out of the shop, I noticed in the window a watch identical to mine: Omega De Ville, *costing over £2,000.* I could hardly believe my eyes! I went to a shop at the top end of town and got a battery and strap for £15.

That evening was a missions meeting, so I wore my new watch with pride and felt like King of the World with a two-grand watch on my wrist! The Missions Director, Peter Corney, said he wanted to stand down after many years of service. I felt God say to me, "This is your inheritance. Like the watch, it's been waiting for this time." What a confirmation of God's plan for me!

The next Sunday, my mum had a prophetic word for me, saying there was a parallel road that I could take; if I did, I would be amazed at where God would take me. I knew that the parallel road God was speaking of was church missions running alongside Guitar Aid missions.

I shared this with Pastor Aran, and he was delighted and invited me to join them each Monday morning for the Riverside team prayer and study time. I told Aran I wanted missions to be accessible and affordable.

In the two years following this, more than 50 people from our church went on their first mission. On our first venture, we took 21 people from our church on a mission to Poland at a cost of £100 for young people and £150 for adults. Thanks to Wizzair and careful planning, the trip came under budget.

Take the Next Step

I'm 19 years old and a member of a small worship band called Sunrise. A few days ago, I received an awesome 12-string guitar from Guitar Aid. I want to say thank you. I love my new guitar. I love its appearance, its sound and every tone I can play on it. Simply, it's perfect! I really like what you do. Thank you for your generosity and kindness. I'm so thankful. This gorgeous gift I was given can help me be a better worship leader. Be blessed in your ministry and let it grow. May the Holy Spirit be with you.

Romana Grolmusova
Slovakia

Take the Next Step

8

The Caribbean and Kenya

We had arrived in Cuba, and as we got to Passport Control, the computers crashed, slowing things down to a snail's pace. We watched on the TV screen the riots and looting in Albania, so thankful we had changed our trip from Albania to Cuba. We proceeded slowly through as the Cuban soldiers checked the passports by hand. John was with me, and also Lea, the brother of a pastor from Jamaica. They got through no problem, but for some reason the soldiers held me up.

"Why are you nervous?" they yelled at me.

"Because you are shouting!" was my reply.

"Why are you shaking?" they asked.

"Because you are pointing a gun at me!" was my reply.

When we finally got through, we were met by the wonderful Pastor Hector Hunter. He looked at Lea and asked, "What are you doing here? Your name is on every computer not to be allowed in the country!"

We told him the miracle of how the computers had crashed just as we arrived. That was the first of many great things that God did on our visit to Cuba.

How it all started

As young people, we always went to the AOG conference, where on one occasion we met a pastor called Veron Kinkead. He was from Jamaica. I spoke to him about the fact that John and I played guitar in our church.

"What style of music do you play?" he asked.

Style? I had never heard of style!

"I play lead and John plays rhythm!" I replied.

Just prior to one of our many trips to Romania, Veron happened to be in Exeter visiting our parents. He prayed for us as we set off and said, "You must come to Jamaica one day." Our passion was to help the persecuted church, especially those under Communist repression, so when Veron said, "We are also taking aid to Cuba and visiting churches there," that sealed it for us; one day we would go to Jamaica and Cuba.

At this time, it was very difficult to go directly to Cuba from the UK. It was impossible to go to Cuba from the USA as they had no diplomatic relations with the Americans; Fidel Castro was very much against the capitalist system, Cuba being a strong Communist country. A few years later, however, we set off with 16 guitars in response to the request.

Jamaica

On our flight out to Jamaica, we were delayed and then informed that, due to the late departure, we would miss the connecting flight from Florida to Jamaica; unfortunately, we would have to make an overnight stop in Miami. Most of the people on the plane were upset. John and I could see nothing unfortunate about having to stop over in the USA! We enjoyed every minute of it.

Our destination in Jamaica was St Elizabeth, a quiet rural area, far from the hustle and bustle of the tourist scene. We loved our time staying in the home of Veron and Claire. The local church, Crossroads, was just a short journey away. I was able to host guitar lessons there with the young people. On the final evening, a young girl, Tenisha, came up to me and said, "Sir, I'z-a gonna miss you!"

We met up with Junior Rutty, a well-known Christian musician who had his own radio station. John and I were able to share our testimony on the radio while we were there. Junior Rutty teased me, "Hey, Whitey, you've got no rhythm!" I wasn't racially offended by his comment; I knew that, compared to them, we really did have no rhythm! We were so thankful we had made connections and built a relationship with Veron over the years, and look back at our time in Jamaica and Cuba with fond memories.

Cuba and Hector Hunter

Jamaica was amazing, but it was really Cuba that had caught our vision. There would be three of us going there: me, John and Veron's brother Leaford. We had no problem in Jamaica purchasing a visa to visit Cuba, and we set off in the smallest plane I have ever seen, arriving at Havana to be met by soldiers with machine guns. It was very intimidating, and led to the experience at the Passport Control shared at the beginning of this chapter.

It is not very often that you get the chance to sit and listen to great men of God like Hector Hunter. He told us of the many times he had been arrested, beaten, stripped naked and put in prison for his faith. As we prepared to share in his church, he explained that if the secret police were to come to that service, there would be consequences for him to face for allowing us to speak. I remember him holding both my hands and praying for God to anoint me in all I do, especially in the work of Guitar Aid. Many times since, as I repair or set up a guitar for sending somewhere, I think of that wonderful prayer that Hector prayed over me.

Just before we had left Exeter for Cuba, our friend Shirley Clear had given us a letter addressed to "Maria, Havana". She told us she had met this woman the year before, that she worked for a church and that God would show us who to give it to! As we sat in Pastor Hector Hunter's office in Havana, we felt we should ask him about the letter and we explained that we knew next to nothing about Maria.

Hector looked at us strangely, then shouted, "MARIA!" at the top of his voice.

From the next office, a lady appeared, and we asked her if she knew Shirley from England. She replied, "Oh, Shirley! My friend Shirley!" So we gave her the letter.

Pastor Hector told us afterwards that Maria is one of the most common names in Cuba... Just another day in the life of a missionary!

The persecuted church and a special anointing

Everywhere we went in Cuba, it seemed like we were being followed. The pastor's son said that it was normal for them. It was a time when it was really hard for Christians to get into Cuba, but bringing guitars "for educational purposes" seemed to be acceptable. For them, being a Christian meant great sacrifice. On our way over, we read an article in an American Christian magazine saying it was impossible to go to Cuba, yet here we were!

Our first meeting with the believers in Cuba was amazing. Young people arrived on what looked like cattle trucks. Soon the outside of the church was packed with about 1,000 people there. And when the worship started, it was incredible. The anointing felt like rain coming down.

I asked the Lord, "What is this?"

I felt the reply was, "This is my anointing for the persecuted church. You are only receiving it because you are here."

Back to Jamaica

We left Cuba with many memories and flew back to Jamaica. Stopping off for Jerk Chicken was a must. It seemed like every street corner had a huge loudspeaker permanently situated there, pumping out reggae music at a volume that would not have been tolerated anywhere else, but this was Jamaica. Our hosts said, "Before you go, you must go to the market in Montego Bay."

We were happy to see the market, but totally shocked when Junior Rutty dropped us off and said, "I'll pick you up here in two hours' time." Oh dear! Nice though it would be to sample the genuine Mo Bay culture, we weren't too happy to be two white boys among a people, place and culture we didn't know. Sure enough, it wasn't long before we took a wrong turn and ended up in a blind alley, only to be confronted by a man with a knife demanding money from us. John quickly threw the change he had on the floor; then, as the man stooped to pick it up, we legged it in a manner that won John the title of Junior Champion for the county of Fife in Scotland.

We came home from the Caribbean with many memories, but also a few things we would have gladly left behind. The mosquitoes must have liked our fresh English blood; I counted 125 mozzie bites when I got home from the trip.

Kenya – our first time in Africa

We were contacted by some of our friends in the Elim churches, saying that the guest speakers at their General Conference were from Africa. They wanted to know if they could have some guitars to take back with them, our friends having told them about Guitar Aid. We gave them the guitars they needed, and it wasn't long before we had an invitation from one of them.

Bishop Simon Githigi invited us to his church in Nairobi. John and I were only too pleased to accept the offer and start planning the trip. We arrived in Nairobi to be joyfully met by Bishop Simon, who we then realised was the head of the Elim churches in Kenya. One of the first things he asked us was if either of us had been to Tanzania. Being our first time in Africa, the answer was obviously no. Simon had some English missionary friends in Arusha, Tanzania, who were going back home. He wanted to say goodbye before they left and also thought it would be an excellent opportunity for us to see more of Africa.

So we set off on a five-hour bus drive. We sat on the back row of the bus, watching them put a plank of wood across the aisle of the seat in front of us in order to get more people in. As that row filled, another plank was put across the next aisle, until the whole bus was jammed full of people. We were completely stuck where we were, with no chance of getting out until they said we could.

Fortunately, they stopped midway for food and the toilet. To our surprise, the stop was in the middle of the Maasia territory with real Maasai warriors roaming around. This was more than we could have imagined. We got back on the bus and now realised why there were so many planks of wood.

It was lovely to meet up with the English missionaries. They were very keen to show us Africa at its best and decided we should go on a safari with them. This was no ordinary safari – nothing organised, no limits to where we would go, just locals who knew the area, showing us where all the animals lived. I loved seeing giraffes in the wild, dozens of them grazing and roaming around.

The missionaries made us aware of the most dangerous animal in the jungle. We naturally thought lions, but no, the animal that kills the most people is a hippo. They explained, "Never get between a hippo and the water. A hippo can run as fast as a car and nothing gets between him and the water!"

We returned to Nairobi in time to preach in the Sunday services at Simon's church. The next day, we went to share at the Bible College. Bishop Simon explained to us that many of the students were refugees and had only recently escaped the genocide that was taking place in Rwanda. Meeting these young men was a humbling experience; we listened intently as they shared their narrow escapes and the horrific scenes they had witnessed and run from. They told us there was no way of hiding their identity as the Tutsi tribe had long, pointed noses, completely different from the Hutu people who had wide, flat noses.

It was a joy to leave guitars with them. They were received with absolute joy and enthusiasm, from people who had lost everything. The hospitality we were given by Bishop Simon and his wife Beatrice was excellent. Kenya had a real impact on us.

One thing I had to do before leaving was, of course… get a flag! We soon realised on this first visit to Africa that we were not as streetwise as we thought. We went shopping in Nairobi with Beatrice, and she told us to meet her in a specific place after one hour. We were free to explore this new environment. We returned an hour later to the meeting place and stood waiting for her. Then a young man came up to us.

"Hi guys," he said, "how are you doing? It's so good to see you again!"

We immediately thought he must have been in the meeting we had spoken at the previous day. He did look kind of familiar to us.

"What are you doing here?" he asked, and we told him that we were waiting for Beatrice.

He spoke nicely to us and said he had to go, so we shook hands and said goodbye.

Five minutes later, he came back. "I've just seen Beatrice, and she is buying some food for your meal tonight. She is $20 short of what she needs; she asked me to see if you can help her."

We passed over the money and then, as he disappeared into the crowd, we realised what we had done! We had been well and truly conned!

From that time onwards, whenever anyone suspicious approached us, we would say, "We met your brother in Nairobi." That seemed to always scare them off.

"

Guitar Aid is doing a great service in providing instruments to churches and individuals who otherwise would not be able to afford them. In our churches, it has helped enrich our praise and worship to God.

Pastor Veron Kinkead
General Superintendent, AOG
Jamaica

Take the Next Step

9

Further trips to Eastern Europe

On one of our trips with George Ridley, we stopped off in Budapest. He told us we were going to meet the best evangelist in the whole of Hungary, Janos Andelic. As soon as we met Janos, we knew we were going to be friends. He was born one day before John. We gave Janos photos of our family and promised that the next time we came to Hungary we would visit him. Janos kept those photos in his Bible, believing we would fulfil our promise...

The Arrow

Each time we went to Romania, we would travel through Hungary in both directions. We did fulfil our promise to Janos and returned with guitars as we had said. This was the start of a lifelong friendship with him and his family. Through this friendship we have travelled the length and breadth of the country, giving many guitars and helping raise the level of worship.

At one time, I was having weekly chats over a coffee with interns at our church. Each week I would share one truth that had helped me in my Christian life so that I could encourage them. I asked Janos if he had one specific thing that I could share with them and he said yes. "Christian ministry, and especially leading worship, is like an arrow. The point is your personal skill; the shaft is your character; the feathers are God's direction. You need all three to hit the target." He explained that without character, you could have skill and God's direction, but you would be off target. If you had no natural ability, you could not penetrate the target as your point would be dull. If you had talent and character, but lacked direction from God, you would also miss. "So, to be on target, you need skill, character and God's direction." I have been able to share this truth many times over the years, always making reference to Janos, who first shared it with me.

Poland and Pastor Wieslaw

On our first trip to Albania, we met Pastor Wieslaw Ziemba from Poland. I remember him sharing with the young people, "Don't let anyone despise your youth." He was really passionate about sharing the love of Jesus. We said to him that we would visit him if we passed through.

It was not long before he got in contact with us and a steady flow of guitars went to Poland. Being one of the closest Eastern European countries, we quite often went there for a weekend and got back home having only taken a couple of days' holiday from work.

Once, I was asked to sing in Wieslaw's church. I did a worship song using a programmed drum machine to play along. It seemed to go down well until I met one lady at the end of the service. She came up to me and said, "For the young people this is wonderful. For me it is awful!" Suffice to say, I didn't use the drum machine there again.

We had many precious times on our travels, connecting, building relationships and returning over many years.

On the Sunday of the Poland trip, we joined together with Pastor Wieslaw for a 'day of prayer' event. What a thrill to join along with 600 other Christians to pray and worship God. Our team was asked to do a couple of songs at the event, and I noticed the bass player there was using a very old Guitar Aid instrument. I was so glad I had given Wieslaw a new bass the previous day.

The bass player said, "I know you," and what he then said really impacted me. "I remember when I was a little boy, you used to come in a Land Rover and bring guitars to Poland."

It made me realise just what an impact years of giving guitars had made. Here was a young man in his twenties who had obviously been influenced by our visits. "When I was a young boy..." I wonder how many more young people we can influence for the kingdom of God. I also learned that the bass had been used for worship every week since we had given it to them so many years ago.

Eastern European tours

For many years, our commitment was to make a Land Rover trip to Eastern Europe towards the end of each year. John and I had such a great partnership. He was able to raise funds to take aid to the orphanage in Romania, we would plan to visit as many countries as possible on the way, and on the way home we would give guitars. A typical route would be to first visit Gianni and Angela, missionaries to Austria. Then we would travel to Poland and stay with Pastor Wieslaw. From there we would go to the Czech Republic, meeting up with Jarek, who we were introduced to at the IBTI Bible College, and from there on to Zilina, Slovakia, to meet up with Stanislav, a friend of Wieslaw. After that we would stay with Marian Lipovsky at the ranch in Králova Lhota, that has been purchased by Youth For Christ as a Christian centre, and then the following day we would head down to Hungary. On the way, we would stop off to see Miro Toth, who was also on the Albania mission, for a coffee, before arriving in Békéscsaba to spend time with Janos.

This all shows how we built up our many contacts in Eastern Europe over a period of many years. On the way home from Romania, we would often travel south, taking in Serbia and Croatia before heading home. Because we did this journey most years for over 25 years, our friends in Eastern Europe knew they could depend upon us to return. Most of these trips involved John, me and Terry Harris, who knew more about vehicles than we did.

One time we took John Bray, a long-time friend, and former member of 'Life Explosion' Christian rock band. John Bray and I really enjoyed being able to play together in so many different settings, from an outdoor event in Romania to playing in the synagogue in Osijek.

We stayed in the homes of many people during those long trips. We were also given the opportunity to preach and share in many churches in Eastern Europe, and in true Guitar Aid style, we never went anywhere without leaving guitars to encourage young people in praise and worship.

We did cause a stir in some places we visited. We parked the Land Rover in Osijek one time and went for something to eat. On returning, we saw crowds gathered round the vehicle. It turned out that we had parked the vehicle with the back corner crossing the tram lines. The whole city tram system ground to a halt, waiting for the crazy Englishmen to move their vehicle. We were given an on-the-spot fine. Thankfully, it was well within our ability to pay. Since then, we have always made sure that we look for the tram lines when parking.

Open doors in Bosnia, Croatia and the Balkans

We knew that when God had called us to missions, he was going to open doors in Eastern Europe. This was just after the war in the former Yugoslavia. We were desperate to make contact with people in that area, because we wanted them to know that people in the UK had been praying for them. Understandably, there was a reluctance for those involved in missions to share their contacts.

We had a stopover in Hannover on one of our trips. When we met the pastor, he started talking about his missionary in Bosnia.

"Do you have contacts there?" we asked.

"Yes, of course, I will ring them..." Soon, "Hi, Peter! I have some friends from England that want to bring you guitars."

"Hi, Peter!" I said, and continued to make contact with my new friend Peter.

When we eventually went to Croatia and met him, we found out this was Peter Kusmic, an international speaker, greatly respected and honoured in World Pentecostal circles – and he was our friend!

One of the places in Croatia that left an impression on us was Vukovar. Driving through the town, the evidence of the war was everywhere; the iconic image of the bombed-out cooling tower stood tall for all to see. The pastor's wife, Maria, had been in the same youth group as our friend Janos from Hungary. Maria told us how difficult it was during the war. The town had been constantly shelled, and all they could do was hide in the basement for safety. She told us that in the middle of the night, they would venture out to collect grass, as that was all they had to eat. This conflict set neighbour against neighbour. One lady in the church lost her husband during the war; she found it difficult to forgive the neighbour who had killed her husband. Things came to a head when the same man came to church, totally broken by what had happened, seeking forgiveness and giving his life to the Lord. The pastor spoke to the lady about her bitterness and encouraged her to forgive. Difficult though it was, she found a release in her spirit when she softened her heart and followed the example of Jesus. What a testimony of grace and forgiveness to now see them in the same room worshipping God!

A journey of surprises through Bosnia

Shortly after the war in Bosnia, we visited the Bible College at Osijek a few times and always enjoyed looking around the shops there. One day, we walked past a certain shop and Terry saw a piece of flexible plastic pipe.

"Oh look," he said to us. "That piece of pipe might be handy!"

More to humour him than anything else, we said, "Let's go and buy it." So we did.

That evening we slept well, knowing the next day we would be off to Bosnia. We started off early in the morning at Osijek in the far end of Croatia, then we drove to the river crossing between Croatia and Bosnia. It was a misty morning when we arrived at the makeshift ferry – and as we looked across the water, we saw nothing but mist. It was a very precarious crossing on what seemed little more than a glorified raft! As we approached the other side, it is difficult to describe the sheer intensity of military activity. Everywhere you looked there were military vehicles, jeeps, tanks, helicopters – you name it, it was there. We seemed to be forever in a convoy with UN and military vehicles. At one point, we had a line of vehicles and tanks in front of us, a line of vehicles and tanks behind us and helicopters flying overhead. You would think this would make you feel safe, but I can assure you it didn't! The roads across the mountains were steep, winding and spectacularly beautiful. At one point, it was so steep that our engine started to overheat. We carried on for a while, the engine still very hot, so Terry decided to look under the bonnet. One of our water pipes had sprung a leak.

"Remember that piece of pipe I bought?" Terry said. "Well, I think it's just the right size to replace the damaged pipe." And it was!

We were so glad Terry had been prompted to buy that odd piece of pipe in Osijek.

We passed many beautiful, Swiss-style villages, but everywhere we went it was the same story: lovely homes reduced to rubble by the ravages of war. Spending a whole day driving, seeing the destruction from one end of the country to the other, was something I could never forget.

The day before this, Peter Kusmic had given us his book entitled *Bosnia, Hope in the Ashes.* As we arrived in Mostar, mentally and physically exhausted, we went straight to the church meeting and saw hope. Children and young people praised God as if nothing had happened. I looked out of the church window and saw nothing but devastation; yet inside, I saw that hope.

That evening, I walked across the river Neretva over a wooden makeshift bridge that was next to where the magnificent Bridge of Mostar had stood. What was left of the bridge lay in pieces in the water below.

The sights and sounds made me think of home. We had three boys at that time. I had wanted two children, Liz had wanted four, and so we had settled for three as a compromise! But after all I had seen that day, after what I had witnessed in Mostar, I thought to myself, "All Liz wants is the chance to have another child," and at that moment I decided, "We will try for a girl one more time, and we will call her Neretva, named after the river that flowed through Mostar." I phoned Liz and told her what I was thinking, but she said, "No daughter of mine will be called Neretva!" Well, it happened, we had the girl, but Becky will always be grateful to Liz that she overruled me on the choice of names!

Turkey

Sometimes we receive invitations from missionaries and have to decide how we are going to respond. Often we will arrange for guitars to be sent as a result of the request, other times we will feel compelled to go and visit them. We had such a request from missionaries in Turkey. Here was a country with a small minority of Christians that needed encouragement. We agreed to go and made our plans. Little did we know at that time, however, that we would be going to an earthquake zone.

A few weeks before we went to Turkey, they had some of the worst earthquakes they have had in that area. Checking it was all over, we agreed to still go. We arrived in what had become a disaster area. Our experience in Armenia with those who had suffered the earthquake there would prove to be a help here. What an experience, to sit alongside families too frightened to return to their homes, now living in tents. We prayed with them, took supplies from the local church and tried to encourage them the best we could.

We visited Golcuk, where the earthquake had been at its worst. The main street on the coast had literally disappeared into the sea. The sight of the street lights getting smaller and smaller until they were no more was unforgettable. Graffiti on one of the remaining walls says, 'Golcuk, we love you.'

Our missionary friends told us that of the 12 million living in Istanbul, there were only a few hundred Christians. They told us how much they were persecuted, with the son of one of the church families mysteriously slipping in the shower while on army duty and dying. They also said that right outside the church, a dear sister was deliberately run down and killed after she left the building.

We had seen persecution in many of the countries we had visited, but this seemed quite different. We prepared for that evening's service with a sense of desperation that we needed to encourage them. We had brought quite a few guitars with us on that trip, so we knew they would be appreciated. John felt compelled to go over and over his sermon until he knew it off by heart.

We arrived at church to find 60 people there, ready to worship. It was pointed out to us that the congregation of 60 represented over 10% of the Christians in the city. The worship was outstanding; it was sweet to my ears, especially as they were using the brand new Guitar Aid instruments we had given them. As John got up to preach, suddenly there was a power cut and all the lights went out. They managed to find a few candles so they could continue. It was reassuring to know that John had learned his sermon off by heart, as he shared passionately in that dimly lit room the love of Jesus and how Jesus cared for the persecuted church.

During that trip, we received a message that my dad had gone into hospital having suffered a stroke. When we returned home, we went straight to the hospital to see him. Although he could not communicate at that time, I still visited him regularly. One evening after work, I asked him, "If you can hear me, squeeze my hand," so he did. I promised him that if anything happened to him, I would look after mum. A tear rolled down his face.

Mum said that when he got home and recovered, he would say, "Don't worry, love. You are going to be alright." Later, she added that only eternity will tell how much my promise meant to Dad and to her.

Take the Next Step

"

Guitar Aid is a fantastic way of combining passion for music with passion for justice. This is a great way to make a difference.

Tim Hughes
UK Singer / Songwriter

Take the Next Step

10

A vision ordered by God

> Once when I was in Africa, a brother told me, "With your type of ministry God will always provide." He added, "What God orders, he pays for. If you go out for a meal, you order what you want and then you pay for it. The vision of Guitar Aid is ordered by God; he will provide the finance you need."

Who wants to be a millionaire?

I have a friend, Al, who has written a book on the principles of Kingdom Business. He seems to have a God-given ability to make money! He had heard about Guitar Aid before he came to our church. When we met, our interest in guitars and missions made for the basis of a good friendship. He invited me and Liz round to his home for a meal, and during the meal he made me an offer, "I'd like to help you become a millionaire!"

It didn't take long for me to reply. "Changing my focus would dull my vision for Guitar Aid. You can't cut with a blunt knife or pierce with a dull spear, so to focus now on making money would not be good for me, or Guitar Aid."

He was surprised by my response, but respected it. From that time, and for a period of over two years, he gave £500 a month to Guitar Aid. This enabled us to raise the level of giving and keep the vision clear and simple. Later on, I had the pleasure of taking him on a mission to Macedonia, Kosovo and Albania. He still supports Guitar Aid. He practises what he preaches, blessed to be a blessing.

I thank God for his faithfulness and the many supporters who have caught the vision to bless others with instruments of worship. This has enabled us to give from abundance, which is so different from how things were in the early years. Later on, during the mission Al went on with me, he saw firsthand the impact of our guitars and the fruit of his giving.

The boy raised by monkeys in Uganda

Working full-time as a toolmaker in an engineering firm has allowed me to fulfil my vision for Guitar Aid. It hasn't always been easy though. My work involved working shifts of 6 am to 2 pm and 2 pm to 10 pm. Working the 2 to 10 shift, the 'late shift', was particularly difficult in the summer. Other families would be having an evening BBQ while you were at work.

One evening, I felt particularly down about being in work, so I got on my knees and prayed. "Please, will you show me that you care for me? I need a sign that you are with me. Please, God, show me in a special way," was my request.

When I came home from work, my usual routine was to watch the 10 o'clock news. Liz would always change channels for me if I asked. That evening she was watching a programme about the boy raised by monkeys in Uganda. The programme aimed to establish the facts of what had actually happened. When John (the real name of the boy) was four years old, he had witnessed his father kill his mother. He was so frightened that he ran off into the jungle and lived there for the next three years. During this time, he was brought up by monkeys in the jungle; they treated him as one of their own, and in fact he acted like one of them. He walked around on all fours, had body hair all over and made sounds like them. When he was spotted, some missionaries tried to get him. The band of monkeys he was with fiercely tried to protect him, throwing things at them. When they eventually got John, they had the long process of teaching him to act like a normal little boy of seven years of age; they had to teach him to eat properly, to talk and to walk upright. After establishing the facts, the programme tried to find out where he was now. This had all happened 20 years ago, so they were now looking for a 27-year-old young man.

By this time, I didn't care about watching the news. I was getting engrossed in the programme Liz had started watching. Where could he be now? The reporter eventually found him, surrounded by a group of people on the streets of Kampala, playing a guitar. As they got closer, I could hardly believe my eyes; the guitar he was playing had 'Guitar Aid' on the headstock – a blue 'Guitar Aid' instrument! How incredible that one of our guitars has helped a boy that had such a difficult start to life! I was so surprised that I called one of my sons to see if we could rewind the programme for me to take a picture of the guitar, which we did.

It made me realise you never know how far your influence will go. God had answered my prayer in a spectacular way.

I sent an email to the presenter of the programme, telling her about me seeing one of our guitars. She replied, "That's absolutely fantastic! Thank you for getting in touch. Meeting John was a real privilege, he's been through so much and his resilience and enthusiasm for life and people isn't dimmed one bit. Cool guy, and he loves that guitar. His guardian, Paul, described how John guards his most important possessions: a couple of books, his clothes and the blue guitar."[5]

One day, I would love to go back to Uganda and meet John with the purpose of giving him a new guitar. We had planned such a trip in 2020, but Covid got in the way and stopped us at that time.

Slovakia, Marian and Campfest

The first time we went to Slovakia, we visited Stanislav in Zilina. Stanislav was a friend of Wieslaw who we met in Albania. When Stanislav heard our vision to give instruments and raise up worship leaders, he said, "There's someone you must meet: Marian Lipovsky, the National Director of Youth for Christ."

The next time we went to Slovakia, we met Marian and immediately became friends. I remember the first time going into the Youth for Christ office, which had a big steel padded door to keep things secure. As the years passed, Marian would share with us his vision for Slovakia and Campfest.

On one visit, we met in a café and Marian excitedly told us of the possibility of buying a ranch for Campfest. We slowly saw that vision materialise. Marian came to Riverside Exeter for one of our Guitar Aid celebration weekends. As a result of this, he invited our Riverside Worship Band to take part in Campfest. After years of hearing about it, I was finally going to see Campfest for myself. I ended up staying for one

---

[5] Mary-Anne Ochota, presenter of 'Raised Wild'; Discovery network

night in one of Campfest's log cabins. Great for one night – but one of these cabins was home for Marian and his family for two years!

On another visit, there was a worship conference and the presence of God was so strong. I asked Marian, "Who was the guy who led the worship?"

"That's Brano. He's a Catholic priest," was his reply.

Brano impressed me with his ability to flow with the Spirit.

Each time someone gave me something a bit special for Guitar Aid, I would immediately think, "This is for Slovakia."

"

Being able to express my deep prayers in song, on a perfect guitar, is for me touching the heavens. I am convinced that Guitar Aid is bringing heaven to earth for many people. Thank you, Dave, for your faithfulness in your vision and duty! Thank you for my guitar as well – you fulfilled my dreams, my friend.

Brano Letko
Worship Leader, Campfest
Slovakia

Take the Next Step

11

Africa

A friend of ours in Exeter – Lesley Curd – was involved with a mission to Tanzania and had taken a team from Exeter to visit them. They had invited a few of them to visit Exeter in return. And so I met Abel, the leader of the team from Tanzania. He came to my home and to where I kept the guitars.

At this time, Guitar Aid didn't have many instruments, as each time we went on a mission we took all we had. At the time of Abel's visit, I had an Ovation guitar hanging up; I was keeping it back for a special occasion.

"Is it possible to have this guitar?" Abel asked.

The thought went through my mind, "If not now, then when? If not him, then who?"

I realised, now was the time and Abel was the man, so I gave Abel my very best guitar. The principle of giving with generosity was already being established. Giving this instrument led to us being invited to Tanzania.

Tanzania and David Livingstone

We took 16 guitars with us on our first visit. The train ride from Dar es Salaam to Tabora was quite an experience. We were given a compartment with two bunk beds; space was definitely at a premium! The triangular shape of the guitars fitted perfectly behind where the door opened. Placed one on top of each other, the 16 guitars reached the roof with less than an inch to spare!

The train ride took 30 hours, so we prepared to make this compartment our home for the next day or so. At each station, we were met by hordes of people trying to sell anything they could. There were many stations along the way, so we soon got used to this routine. What took us by surprise was, at night they came and knocked on our door to give us a stick.

"What is that for?" we asked.

"To keep the robbers out!" was the reply.

Apparently, the stick was used to wedge the window shut. At first, we had thought perhaps we were to fend off robbers with the stick!

Having been brought up in Scotland, our thoughts went to David Livingstone during this journey. We wondered if he had travelled this way. We loved the experience of travelling so far into Africa. Each town we went through raised the same question: "Did David Livingstone come this way?"

We arrived in Tabora to be met by Elias Shija. The first Sunday at his church was amazing! How they worshipped in Africa! The rhythm, the enthusiasm, the sounds; it all touched us deeply. Can you imagine our surprise when, after the meeting, Elias asked, "Would you like to visit the place where David Livingstone lived?"

Wow – to think the whole journey we had been on was the same way he had come! We stood in awe at the place that had been his home and thought back to the times in school we had dreamed of following in the footsteps of David Livingstone – and here we were at what was his home.

While we were in Tanzania, they took us to the equator line. This is marked by a large post and a sign. On one side of the road, the water swirls round in a clockwise direction; on the other side of the road, the water swirls in an anti-clockwise direction. It is quite strange to see this firsthand.

While we were in Tanzania, we had the privilege of taking part in a crusade. The sea of faces seemed to go on and on. Never before had we seen a people so eager to hear the gospel. Tanzania left such an impression on us that we determined we would return there again.

Ask and it will be given

During the long train ride of over 600 miles from Dar es Salaam to Tabora, we had time to think, and I reflected on how Abel had found the courage to ask for the guitar he had needed. During the trip, we thought about how we needed a newer Land Rover and more guitars, having given most of our stock away. God prompted us to think about a wealthy man in our church who had promised that one day he would help us. Those words, "If not now, when? If not us, then who?" came flooding into our thoughts. We decided on that journey that we would talk to him when we got home.

After returning from Africa, we took a gift to the brother's house. We went to his home in fear and trembling, but sure of the fact that God had spoken to us. We shared our vision with him then and, with hearts pounding, asked, "If not now, when? If not us, then who?"

The response was instant. "I would like to give you £10,000 so you can use £5,000 to buy a new Land Rover and £5,000 to buy guitars."

This gift allowed us to move forward in a way that would have otherwise been impossible.

Dad's passing

Saying goodbye as we set off on a mission is never easy, but sometimes it's harder than others; like the time when Liz had a fall with our youngest, Daniel, when he was about five months old, and he'd broken his leg. Because in those days you had to get a visa to travel, it was not possible for someone else to take my place, so I had to go, leaving Liz with a very difficult situation to cope with. I have a saying about missions: "Missions are usually inconvenient, but rarely impossible."

The hardest of all farewells was when our dad was taken into hospital. We visited him just before we left for the trip. Because we were leaving the country, we took time to say a proper goodbye. We were halfway across Germany when that awful phone call came to say that our dad had passed away.

Benjamin, my son, was with me on that trip. We shared that deeply sad moment as we hugged each other – me realising I had lost my dad, Benjamin realising he had lost his grandad.

In those days, customs were really strict. We had exported a trailer-load of goods and would not be able to take them back to the UK. The quickest way home was to travel to Romania and return immediately when the goods had been delivered. We set up a meeting with all the people we were due to meet up with, explained the situation and then returned home.

To this day, I feel that although my dad has gone, his influence is still here. I also thank God he chose to move to Exeter. I am still able to hear his voice and benefit from his ministry. Mum set up a tape service that recorded each Sunday meeting and gave the cassette tape to people who could not get to the meeting. This tape ministry has meant that now we have literally hundreds of Dad's sermons recorded. Whenever I mention his name, people who knew him respond by saying he had a gentle spirit and was a real 'man of God'.

Keeping promises

We learned very early on in missions that one big principle is, never make promises you can't keep.

One of the first friendships we made was with the Ardiu family, particularly Cassius. We have a saying that we often repeat, 'mates for life'. This has been true with Cassius; we truly have been mates for life. Cassius' parents lived just around the corner from the church. Their home was always in a process of being done up and often resembled a building site.

On my very first visit, someone in our group from another church looked at the work being done on the house and made an observation and a rash promise: "Your windows look like they need replacing; we could do that!"

John and I looked at each other in shock, but Cassius' dad looked in delight! "Multsumesc, multsumesc!" was his response. ("Thank you!" in English.)

We now had a dilemma; a promise had been made that would be very difficult to fulfil. What type of windows – wood or UPVC? Where were we going to get them – the UK or Romania? Who was going to pay for them; who was going to fit them? Were we going to take up valuable space in the lorries with enough windows to complete the house?

This was a valuable lesson in not making promises without thinking the whole thing through. Fulfilling that promise in part became a headache to the church involved.

Osijek in Croatia is one of our favourite places. We made a promise there that we were able to fulfil.

Damir Spoljaric, the head of the Pentecostal churches in Croatia, always looks after us well when we go there. One day, I was sitting in a café there with John and Daniel Darko. Daniel was one of the leaders at the Bible College and was from Ghana; he was married to Meryl, who was from the USA. Daniel invited us to Ghana.

We were not sure what the future held, but we could say with confidence, "If we come to Ghana, we will come to you."

Fast forward a couple of years and Riverside started to plan a mission to Ghana. I was invited, and I remembered the promise I had made to Daniel. I established what the mission involved and realised it would leave no time to see him; therefore, it left me with no option but to say no. I had made a promise to Daniel and I was going to keep it.

A while later, we had an invitation from Daniel: "Please come to Ghana. I want you to be guests at the graduation of the students in the Bible College."

So it was agreed, John and I would go to Ghana.

First time in West Africa

Daniel Darko met us at the airport. In fact, we just missed bumping into Bono from U2, who had arrived the same day as us to attend a charity event that was aimed at reducing poverty in Ghana. I thought to myself, "It would be so good for someone like him to know we are giving guitars to these people in West Africa."

Daniel had a full programme for us that started with giving us an insight into the history of the country. He took us to Cape Coast to see the centre of where the slave trade took place. Our biggest shock was to find it was fellow Africans that had transported the slaves from East Africa to West Africa where they would be shipped out. We were totally shocked at the whole process. It was as if they had had a factory-type system that processed these poor individuals as if they were pieces of meat. John and I wept as we contemplated the misery that this place had experienced in its dark past.

The heat of the day and the emotion hit us hard. Time to cool down with an ice lolly. I took mine out of the wrapper. John didn't. I felt fine; however, John went down with food poisoning and was confined to bed for the next two days.

We could sense that the people in Ghana were God-fearing. Most of the shops had rather strange biblical-type names: 'Shekinah Glory Hair Salon' or 'God Is Good Taxi Service'. Everywhere you looked, you could see the influence of God. We visited the Bible College and were asked to share with the students.

Then my phone rang. It was St Peter's High School in Exeter. "Could you please come and pick up your son, Ben, as he is ill?"

My reply was not what they wanted to hear. "You need to know two things. Firstly, this phone call will cost you a lot of money. Secondly, I am in Africa and can't come to pick Ben up!"

We loved the West African style of worship. The guitars we gave were appreciated so much. I am so glad we kept our promise to Daniel.

Before, we didn't have any instruments, but now we have been supplied with guitars. This will help us so much to worship God, to sing to him and praise the Lord! We want to thank you, thank you and thank you again for providing these nice guitars. We are playing the instruments for Jesus. Thank you and the Lord bless you always.

Pastor Boniface
Principal of Bakuva Bible College
Congo

Take the Next Step

12

From near death to Romania

Four of us had left on a mission to Romania in the Land Rover. I had just finished my driving 'shift', and we had changed over and were heading for Swindon.

As were overtaking a lorry, our vehicle suddenly appeared to go out of control, first swaying one way, then the other. Then all of a sudden it rolled over with the most deafening crash I have ever heard! We totally lost any sense of what was up and what was down.

As the vehicle was rolling I felt like it was the end of my life...

At the hospital

Our usual team with the Land Rover and trailer was me, John and Terry. When Terry was diagnosed with an illness, he had to take a break from missions. John and I thought it would be a good idea if we both chose someone to go on the trip with us. I chose my father-in-law, Mike, who had been on the lorry trips with us; John chose David, who he had been working with. So John, Mike, David and I were in the Land Rover when it rolled over on the motorway.

As I felt my life was ending, I saw a vision of my dad, who had passed away years before.

"It's too soon, son," he said as he looked intently at me.

Immediately everything seemed to grind to a halt... The Land Rover was on its side on the hard shoulder, with the trailer having left the motorway in pieces on the verge.

I climbed out of the place that was once the front window to view the devastation. It seemed like only minutes until we were completely surrounded by emergency vehicles: fire brigade, police, ambulances, they were all there. I was the only one with no injuries.

I heard the police say, "How anyone came out of this alive, I will never know."

Right then, I knew we were in a spiritual battle. We were surrounded by broken goods and boxes from the trailer scattered everywhere. What hit me most was the sight of broken, smashed brand-new guitars. Everything about the scene seemed to say, "You are going nowhere!" I looked at the adjacent field, alongside the motorway, and spiritually I could visualise demons dancing and laughing. They seemed to be agreeing, "Nowhere!"

At this point, we were all taken to the Accident and Emergency department of Swindon hospital. The other three had all contacted their wives to say they were coming home. I had not done this. I was the only one in the hospital not to have treatment.

A policeman said to me, "You might be insured for onward travel."

This was music to my ears. I went and found John, who was still being treated, and shared the news. At first, what I was saying didn't seem to sink in. He was thinking of going home and was grateful just to be alive. But by the time John had finished being treated, he had to listen to me as I kept on about "onward travel".

It was now 5 pm and soon everything would be shut. We contacted one hire company, and they said they would come and see us in the next half hour and would sort something out. By the time the other two had been treated, John and I had a plan and a determination to carry on if possible. The vehicle we rented was a 17-seater minibus; it cost £700 which we could claim back from the insurance. By this time, our stuff had been cleared off the motorway and taken to a police storage area. We went to see what was left of our goods, and to our surprise, there was enough good stuff to completely fill the minibus.

Hindered but not defeated, we set off for Romania five hours after what was a near fatal accident. John and the other two had to contact their wives to say they were now going on to Romania; I just had to explain after the event exactly what had taken place.

When we arrived at Romania, we were able to go to a photo shop and get digital pictures of the crashed vehicle printed on A4 paper. Everyone could see the miraculous escape we had made. Most humbling of all was that the church in Lipova decided to take up an offering to start a fund for a new Land Rover for us!

What did the men from England say?

We always enjoy meeting up with our friend Viorel from Deva when we go to Romania. He is a great advocate of the fivefold ministry – prophets, pastors, apostles, evangelists and teachers. When we first met Viorel, his home was full of orphan children that he had taken in off the street. He was a great visionary and a builder by trade. One time when we met him, he was at a point where he didn't know what to do next as he had completely run out of finances for his many projects. He had finished the church and orphanage in Deva and wanted to show us the other projects that had been put on hold, waiting for the money to continue.

Our first stop was Alba Iulia, where we were shown a massive plot of land that Viorel had bought. He asked us to pray about it. John and I felt uneasy; the area was very large – so much land. We prayed for wisdom as to what to do with it, and when we had finished praying, both John and I told him, "Sell the land."

We then travelled on to Hunedoara to pray over another piece of land. This place excited us, as it had a prominent position overlooking the town. It had so much potential and was right where the people were. We suggested that the money from the sale of the land at Alba Iulia could finance everything he needed to do in this brilliant place.

When Viorel got home, his wife asked him, "What did the men from England say?"

He replied, "Sell the land in Alba Iulia."

In due course, the land was sold. A smaller piece of land was purchased and the rest of the money bought them a JCB. The JCB was in such demand that now Viorel and his son Sebi were constantly bringing in finances from the use of the equipment.

On the land in Hunedoara stands an orphanage and a magnificent church building. From the day they sold the land in Alba Iulia, they have never looked back. It was a word in due season.

John and I had the privilege of being invited to the opening of the new church. What a celebration that was! We were both able to share in that service, giving God the glory for what he had done. I presented them with a special guitar to mark the occasion. We often look back to the time when we stood on the plot of land praying and believing this was the right place for a church and orphanage to serve the community. The services are often online. It gives us great pleasure to see how the vison Viorel had has come to pass.

New improved transport and the 1,500th guitar

Within five months of losing our Land Rover, we were back on the road with a new trailer and a five-year-old Land Rover Discovery. The change from a Defender to a Discovery was quite significant and much more comfortable. As we drove the 3,500 mile round trip to Eastern Europe, we thanked God many times for our new vehicle.

This trip coincided with us giving our 1,500th guitar. It was the reaction to the first guitar given in 1990 that had inspired the vision for Guitar Aid. It seemed a good idea to find the person who received that guitar and present him with the 1,500th guitar. One of our Romanian friends recognised him from an old photo and arranged for us to meet up.

What a blessing to meet Gabriel again! We relived the night in 1990 when he had left the church whooping with delight, holding the guitar above his head and thanking God for the provision of his own instrument. Gabriel is still actively involved in youth work.

Four-wheel-drive

One time, we visited Romania with Pastor Janos. We had flown to Hungary for a weekend of ministry and thought it would be good to go over to Romania to see our friends there. Terry had come on this trip with us, so the four of us were dropped off at the border and were met by our friends from the orphanage. Later that day, we would be picked up by Janos' son David.

While we were at the orphanage, Janos noticed four alloy wheels with nice tyres on them. He asked the director of the orphanage what they were being used for, and found that they were no longer needed. Janos said they were exactly the right size for a vehicle he had. It was agreed that Janos could have them. The only problem was getting them back to Hungary. As there were four of us, we agreed to take one wheel each. We were dropped off at the border, ready for David to pick us up.

We thought it would be funny to make the formation of a car with the four wheels, so we jogged up to the border guards saying, "We came to Romania with a whole car; this is all we have left." They saw the funny side of it, and when they stopped laughing, they gladly let us through. They then realised they had forgotten to check our passports and had to call us back before we finally went through to Hungary.

I often wonder what others looking on must have thought, seeing four grown men acting as kids, pretending to be a car! We often look back and laugh at some of the things we did during the many years of travelling through Eastern Europe.

Activetate! Activetate!

For many years, Liz and I have gone to Romania in May to have an activity week with the children of the Haven of Hope Orphanage in Lipova. Most days, the children are at school in the morning and eagerly return home at midday to get involved in the activities.

I have the ability to hype up the kids. We march around the orphanage chanting, "Activetate! Activetate!" They love it! We pack as many craft ideas as we can in a box, which also has guitars in it. The weight allowance is 32kg, which is very heavy, so we have no problem packing in whatever we like.

On many of these trips, we have taken our daughter Becky with us. She was the same age as a few of the children there and integrated really well while we were there. One day, Becky was playing along with the children with the rabbits, then later that week we had rabbit for dinner. When Becky asked what it was, we told her it was rabbit. She said, "Rabbit, *bunny rabbit?*" and immediately went to where she had seen the rabbits previously, only to see that they had gone! Yes, it was rabbit, bunny rabbit that we had been given for lunch.

To get from Budapest to Arad, we used a minibus company called Recreation. One time we were in a long queue and the driver was having none of it. He drove off the road, on to a farmer's field and proceeded to overtake the whole queue, driving for miles on the field. Another time, on our way on Recreation, we were stopped by the police. They were very keen to see what was inside everyone's bags. We watched them inspect a family. A teenager had a Nike shoe box, and they asked him what was inside. "Should be shoes," was his reply. Yes, it *should have been* shoes, but this particular box was full of cigarettes! His mother was caught carrying some kind of drugs, so they both had the items confiscated and were given an on-the-spot fine. The police looked at us and asked, "English?" to which we said yes. No problem; they didn't need to check us.

Activity week became a real favourite with the children. Liz loved being involved with them and willingly shared her creative skills. On one activity week, at the weekend when we had free time, our friend Gemma, who we introduced to the orphanage, wanted to have a few days' break. We headed off to Gales, right in the centre of Transylvania. I was given the job of driving Gemma's car, as she didn't feel too well. The rain on the way was torrential. At one point, the windscreen wipers stopped working, so we pulled into a truck stop and found assistance from the lorry drivers, who got us on the way again.

I should not have told Liz that when we first went to that village, you could feel the evil there. In the bedroom, the windows rattled; the family pictures on the wall resembled Dracula. There were two beds, but Liz said, "I don't care how small I have to make myself; I'm sleeping in your bed with you. I'm not sleeping on my own."

Once the first night was over, it was like a girls' club. Gemma, Liz and Dr Julia, who we were staying with, seemed to laugh about everything! By the end of the three days, I started to think they must be laughing at me!

Strange customs

We often encounter customs in different countries that are strange to us. None of these are more peculiar than one custom in Romania that we encountered. We had our daughter Becky with us on this visit, as we were having an activity week with the children from the orphanage.

One morning, while the children were at school, we decided to go to the big Catholic church right at the top of the village. We couldn't believe our eyes when we walked in. The wall in front of us was covered with paintings that had been made by the families who had lost loved ones. The paintings depicted graphically how the people had died: someone lying under a car, another being pulled into farm machinery, another being knocked off a bike, and many others, all depicted with no shortage of blood! It was like a horror scene.

Becky left feeling totally traumatised! We were equally shocked. I am glad that is not a tradition in our country, where dignity is of paramount importance in dealing with such sensitive issues. Safe to say that on future visits, a trip to the Catholic church was not on the agenda!

"

We thank God for the ministry of Guitar Aid. The gift of guitars to the church in Ghana has improved our worship tremendously. We pray the Lord will enlarge the coast of Guitar Aid to be a blessing to many others in the body of Christ.

Rev. James Mensa
Ghana, West Africa

Take the Next Step

LIFE Explosion

What have you got in your hands?

Paul McCartney with the miniature guitar Dave made

John and Dave Sumner

Mission in Romania – old and new forms of transport

Mission in Albania

Armenia

The third Land Rover, fully loaded, in Romania

Mission in Bosnia

Outside the home of Veron and Claire in Jamaica

The church in Hunedoara, Romania

After the earthquake in Turkey

Guitar Aid at IBTI Bible college

Dave with his good friend, Pastor Elias

Minus 16 in Ukraine!

The road accident

Mission in Ethiopia

Mission in India

On Sipaway Island

Giving the 3,000th guitar

Mission in Macedonia

*Dave's parents,
Pastor Fred and Hazel*

Second mission in Egypt

Mission in Togo

Mission in Peru

Chris in recovery

Mission in Belarus

Guitar Aid offices

Dave Sumner and family

13

Cambodia

John and I were on our first bus trip in Cambodia. An hour into our journey, we had just passed a village and noticed a man on a moped travelling on a dirt track, at right angles to the road we were on, heading straight for it. Surely he would stop as he got to the bus freeway? But no, he just kept on going and ended up right in front of the bus. With an enormous crash, his life was taken, just as easily as if he had been a fly on the windscreen.

The noise of the collision was intense, but the driver didn't stop for half a mile. From what we could see, looking back, it appeared that the man's body was a few hundred yards behind us, while the bike itself was still well and truly wedged under the front of the bus. When the bus finally stopped, the driver ran out and carried on running for his life until his figure disappeared into the distance.

Cambodia, our first time in Asia

Our good friend Shirley Clear had made many friends during her missions travels. Jim and Agnes Verner, who are WEC missionaries from Cambodia, were a couple she introduced us to. Jim was from Ireland and had a love of football; Agnes was from Canada and had a God-given gift of being able to organise anything. Jim and Agnes loved our vision to give guitars and didn't hesitate to invite John and me to stay with them in Cambodia.

When we arrived, they had decided we should stay in a room at the girls' school. The idea of this didn't exactly appeal to us. The practicalities were even worse. To visit the toilet along the corridor in the night meant getting dressed in case we bumped into any of the girls staying there. John and I did not get a wink of sleep as our room companions, of the really large beastie variety, were running up and down the walls all night. The sheer size of these horrible black creatures made us shiver.

The next day, we had to have a serious chat with Jim and Agnes. We are not proud, most circumstances we can accept, but if they wanted us to travel the length and breadth of Cambodia, we needed a good night's sleep. For five dollars a night, we were booked into the Hotel Champs-Élysées. What a difference! We have learned on missions, taking care of your own wellbeing is vitally important if you are going to be effective.

This was our first trip to Asia, and we were not quite sure what to expect. We had read many reports of what life was like since the Pol Pot reign of terror. We felt a bit like Joshua and Caleb, because instead of despair, we found a country rich in the anointing of God. It was vibrant with the sound of young people worshipping God in a way that we have rarely seen on any of our travels. The New Life Centre was alive with God's praises. It reminded me of the phrase used in a letter I once received: "The servants are young and they burn." This is certainly true of the youth in Phnom Penh. NLC is totally alive with the presence of God. I wish you could have seen their faces when they received their new guitars.

Guitar lessons in Phnom Penh

Young Life is a youth group working with college students; we had a great time with them. We were able to obtain a couple of amplifiers to go with the guitars they received. Cambodia has had a brutal past, in which death, destruction and persecution were commonplace. This has left the country with 75% of the population under the age of 25. As we left Cambodia, I could not stop the tears rolling down my face as I reflected on what had been a most memorable trip. The word I took to them was from Joshua 3:5: "Consecrate yourselves, for tomorrow I will do amazing things amongst you."

John and I made our minds up that Cambodia was a place we would like to visit again. Jim and Agnes had organised things so well for us; we appreciate having lifelong missionaries like them as friends.

Before we left Cambodia, Jim and Agnes said we should visit the Killing Fields museum. This turned out to be a horrendous experience.

All the atrocities that took place were shown in far too much detail for our minds to take in. We looked in horror at what the people had suffered under the Khmer Rouge and Pol Pot. We visited villages that had been devastated by the sheer scale of killing. The skulls on display would have been measured in hundreds. This was a chilling reminder to us of what the country had been through. We returned home knowing that our instruments were going to be used in worship, to bring healing and hope to a people that had been crushed by evil.

Often we give guitars and it goes unnoticed; other times, it seems that God has a plan for the profile of our work to be raised. We had not long come back from Cambodia when the *Christian Herald* decided to feature the work of Guitar Aid with a full-page story. The title was 'God's guitar man'. I was able to reproduce this article for my newsletter. I'm not sure about such a grand title! I have a copy of the feature on the wall in the Guitar Aid room at Riverside.

The coach accident

On our first trip to Cambodia, our very full itinerary was organised by Jim and Agnes. On our second, we were planning to visit Vietnam, but John's passport only had one page left, so we could leave the country but couldn't return, as entry required a full page visa for both countries. Jim and Agnes suggested we should go north to visit Riksa, a man who had written the book *Tears of My Soul*. They briefed us on travel etiquette in Cambodia and took us to the coach station the next day.

John and I had seats in the second row, right near the front of the coach. We set off completely unaware of the events that were to follow, the story told at the beginning of this chapter.

After the coach driver had run away, we remembered the advice Jim and Agnes had given us and were able to advise other English-speaking travellers of the line we must take: *we saw nothing!* By this time, a large crowd had gathered around the man's body down the road. It was obvious they wanted to kill the driver in an act of revenge. We told everyone to stay on the bus, which turned out to be good advice because in no time at all, the bus was surrounded by angry villagers that wanted revenge for their friend's death. Some of the men had machetes, others had axes. The whole scene was getting ugly and extremely dangerous. Thanks to our advice, everyone on the bus stayed put. When asked, we all said we saw nothing!

After enduring this tension for about an hour and a half, the police finally arrived, much to our relief. It could have been such a different story had we not listened to the advice given.

Two more surprises

We eventually travelled on to Siem Reap, without further incident, where two more surprises awaited us.

One was the town right next to Angkor Wat, one of the wonders of the world. The place was amazing to behold, a kingdom that had been hidden for centuries. The scale of the buildings and temples and the detail of the carvings was something to behold.

The other surprise was Riksa. What a trophy of grace, what forgiveness, what character! As we listened to his story, we openly wept. He told us of the ordeal of being left for dead at the bottom of a pit of villagers and family members. During the night, he had clawed his way to the top and managed to escape to the woods, fleeing to safety. During his months in the woods, Riksa told us that a man in white came and gave him food while he was there. Riksa eventually went to Canada, where he gave his life to Jesus. At first as a Christian, he still struggled with forgiveness, until the time came when he fully and freely forgave those that had killed his family.

The proceeds of the sale of Riksa's book were used to build a school in the village where the massacre had taken place. Amongst those attending that school are the children of the very man who murdered his family.

Never before had we witnessed such grace and forgiveness. Riksa left an impression on us that is still as strong today. His book, *Tears of My Soul*, is well worth reading.

Our craziest journey

When we returned to Jim and Agnes, they had more adventures awaiting us. We were to share at a village about half an hour's drive away. We were taken by car, along with a guitar that would be left at the home group.

Life in the village was very simple, perhaps even primitive. We sat on the floor of the home worshipping with an enthusiastic group of young people. When it was finished, we looked for the car to take us back, only to be shown two small 50cc mopeds that John and I were to travel back on. This was the most crazy journey we have ever made. Cambodian roads are bad enough in a car, but on the back of a moped... well, that's a different story! I was on the second moped following John, and it looked like the rear wheel on John's bike was screaming for mercy under his weight!

We did eventually make it back safely. John and I looked at each other and said simultaneously, "Never again!" We asked one of the young men who had brought us back how old he was. He replied that he didn't know his age or his birthday as both his parents had been killed in the Pol Pot era.

The next meeting was in another village. We had to climb up to the level where the meeting was to take place, as the house was on stilts. Again, John's weight got the better of him, as every time he got up or moved, the house shook!

Cambodia made us thankful for our home and the heritage we have in this country.

Take the Next Step

My name is Fiona; I am 23 years old. I am so grateful for the guitar I got from you and I love it so much; getting it is a dream come true. It's not only been helpful for me but also for my friends, and for my nephew, who uses it at his church during choir practice. The church also uses the guitar during services. I would like to say thank you very much for making my dream come true. The guitar is being used to do great and amazing things, and I give thanks to the Lord for that. May the good Lord continue to bless you abundantly.

Fiona Atim
Watoto Church
Kampala, Uganda

Take the Next Step

14

Friends old and new

Over the years, we have developed an excellent relationship with the guitar importers in Leeds. On one occasion, the MD Dennis Drumm wanted to chat about Guitar Aid. During the conversation, he said, "What you need for your charity is a Patron, a figurehead, someone to add extra credibility to the cause, someone like Sir Cliff Richard."

They approached him on my behalf and the reply we got was quite incredible. During this time, Sir Cliff was backing out of his commitment to charities and refusing to accept offers to be involved. However, on this occasion, he was glad to accept the position of Patron of Guitar Aid.

Sir Cliff has signed a guitar for us, which has pride of place in the Guitar Aid office; he also supplied us with a quote for us to use on our website.

Restoring the imperfect

We read in the Bible how the Lord wanted Jeremiah to learn a lesson from the potter. He saw that the jar the potter was making did not turn out how he had hoped so he crushed it into a lump of clay and started again. The lesson from this is that God can take the imperfect and make it useable for him. Many of our instruments are sold to us as 'seconds or grade B instruments'. Usually, the defect is something that we can fix. In the early days, John and I would try to fix anything. John would take guitars to work and repair them during his lunch break. More recently,

John Bray, who was in Life Explosion band with me, would give many hours helping in this work.

The favourite job was to turn an acoustic guitar into an electro/acoustic with built-in tuner. On one visit to IBTI Bible College, I decided to do this in front of the students. I took an acoustic guitar and played it, explaining that the sound could only fill the room we were in. Then, much to the surprise of the students, I started to make a hole in the side of the guitar with my drill and a saw, and completed the process of fitting a pickup system into the instrument. Once finished, I played the electro acoustic guitar to them. That instrument could now be tuned with the electronic tuner, plugged in and amplified so that the sound could fill a stadium.

"You are like that guitar with what you learn in Bible College," I told the students. "God wants to tune you up and amplify what you have."

John Bray and I had regular times together fixing the guitars we bought from Tanglewood. For a long time, it was every Thursday that we would get together for this. Anything more tricky or technical, John would take home and fix. We have had literally hundreds of guitars from Tanglewood, all of them needing a bit of care and attention. We have become like the potter, taking something imperfect and making it 100% usable for God's kingdom.

Connections from the first Albania trip

The trip to Albania proved to be very significant. Firstly, John Partington was on that trip. A few years later, we were looking for a pastor and I said to my brother John, who was an elder at that time, "Why not invite John Partington?" The rest is history. 'JP', as he was known, led Riverside and saw it grow and prosper. We also met Wieslaw Ziemba and Lubo Hlavacka on that trip, both of whom we met several times on subsequent missions trips. However, we never saw anything of Miro Toth, who had been a young 18-year-old lad on the Albanian trip.

One day in Slovakia, we were watching footage of the most recent Campfest event, when a guy with an 'afro' hairstyle came on and underneath it was Miro Toth!

"Hey, we know him!" John and I exclaimed.

Yes, indeed, it was him. Marian Lipovsky who headed up Campfest told us that Miro was one of the top worship leaders in Slovakia. It was great to meet up with him and chat over a coffee in his hometown of Kosice.

It was even more of a surprise to be signing in to Campfest in 2012 and to bump into the very same Miro Toth! He was leading worship and preaching at the main event that evening. We invited Miro to Riverside Exeter to take a worship weekend. He soon became a big favourite with the people at Riverside, especially the youth.

Hungarian Roma church

Our good friend Janos has taken us the length and breadth of Hungary, giving guitars, preaching and sharing the love of Jesus wherever we go. Many times on missions, we have to move outside our comfort zones and go to places we would not normally think of going. Some of the Roma churches in the north of Hungary fall into that category. Their meetings are wild and exuberant. I see it as a cross between Hillsong and karaoke, Benidorm-style. If you can picture that, you will appreciate how wacky it all seemed to us.

The call for prayer at the end was even more bizarre! We had preached our hearts out and sung with all the enthusiasm we could muster and now was the response time. The first lady in the line asked, "Please pray for me. My husband has run off with his fancy woman and I have put a spell on him. Please pray it works!" Hmm… better think before speaking on that one!

When the next lady came out, John had a feeling and said to me, "Don't look into her eyes." As I prayed through a squint, I could see her pirouette as if she were on ice skates, spinning away from me.

My dad's pastoral advice on these things was, "If you don't know what you are doing, stay away from this sort of thing if possible." I'm not sure we exactly knew what was going on, but God's grace kept us safe.

John's first love for Hungary, begun in the late 80s, has continued to this day. We feel very much at home when we visit Pastor Janos and his family. Each time we go to Hungary, Janos will arrange for us to visit as many churches as possible. Seeing instruments we have previously given being used is something that always inspires me. The simple vision of Guitar Aid has not changed over the years.

Székesfehérvár

We visited the church in Székesfehérvár, which was being held in a small tin hut, the sort of thing that might be used as a garage or a store. Earlier in the day, Pastor Stephen, who led the work there, had shared with us his vision for a new church building. He showed us the plans that he kept in his briefcase and took them everywhere with him. During the service, John spoke on having a dream and believing your dream will become reality. He told the congregation, "Your pastor has a dream," as he shared what the pastor had told us, and he said he would like to pray for this vision.

The pastor came to the front and took out the plans for the new church from his briefcase. We laid them on the floor, and the pastor and his wife knelt down to pray over the plans. John then invited everyone who shared in the vision to come and pray with the pastor. Virtually everyone in the church came forward. It was a time of desperation. We could see how much they needed a new building; the surroundings we were in were very poor, to say the least.

The next time we visited Székesfehérvár, we could hardly believe our eyes! A brand new, state-of-the-art church building was right in front of us. Pastor Stephen told us how the miracle had happened and how our prayers in the old tin hut had been answered.

We have been privileged to see this happen in other places as church-planting has become a high priority of the leaders in Hungary. We are glad to see our instruments being used in these new churches.

Saddleback, California

Rick Warren has written a book, *Purpose Driven Church*. Our pastor was so impressed with it that he decided a team should go out to California to the next conference they were holding in his church at Saddleback, Orange County. As Liz was involved in the children's ministry and I was leading worship at that time, we both got an invitation to go.

As a lifelong surfer, the thought of going to California sounded out of this world. I was so excited at the thought of it. My plan was that I would also take a couple of guitars to give away and help promote the ministry of Guitar Aid. So the team from Exeter set off.

We were told that when we arrived, the first day would be a free day. I had a chat with my friend Al who, like me, enjoyed surfing, and along with his wife Heather and Liz, we set off on the Pacific Coast Highway in search of surf. We arrived at Newport Beach, hired a couple of boards, and within 24 hours of landing in California we were surfing Newport Beach. Classic!

The church there in California had arranged for our accommodation. We had a brief stay with a rather strange young man. He kept batteries in the fridge, answered the phone in our bedroom sitting at the bottom of the bed *while we were in it* and behaved in a manner that left us uncomfortable, so we were moved. We were then placed very much upmarket, with Dr Rock, a drummer, and foot specialist; staying with the rich and famous. He lived in a gated community, in a very grand house, complete with swimming pool, gym and cinema room. In spite of the opulence and glamorous lifestyle, it just didn't seem to impress me. I guess the thought that comes to mind is, "…godliness with contentment is itself great wealth."[6] The American dream is not for me. Having said that, I loved every minute of our time in California and fulfilled something I had wanted to do since I was a child listening to the Beach Boys.

The conference was amazing, and we loved Rick Warren's vision, generosity and character. The guitars we took were also put to good use. At the missions meeting, two churches were selected to have the instruments. The worship leaders there loved what we are doing with Guitar Aid.

Saddleback Church is on a massive campus. The main auditorium is the biggest building there, and around the campus there are other venues for church. When the congregation arrives on a Sunday, they have the choice of which style of service they like. This ranges from traditional with hymn to overdrive led by a rock band! At the appropriate time, they all hear the same sermon from Rick as it is relayed by video to the various venues. Rick is live in the main auditorium.

This concept was completely new to us. When our church grew to a size that was too big for our main hall, we adopted the Saddleback method, with the main service called 'Broadband' and the smaller venue called 'the wave'. I enjoyed leading the wave; this service allowed for a

---

[6] 1 Timothy 6:6

less formal approach, making it easier for the congregation to be involved.

Other musicians

On the return flight from Los Angeles, Liz and I met Darius Danesh, who was famous for appearing on Pop Idol. Darius loved the concept of Guitar Aid. His response was immediately to say, "Give someone a fish and you give them a meal, give someone a fishing rod and they can get many meals, but give someone a guitar and soon you will have a musician!" As a result of that meeting, we became friends and visited his home in London a few times. We worked together on what became the 'Darius Guitar Aid guitar'. He signed the sound-hole label and had his logo next to the Guitar Aid one.

Soon after returning from America, we met up with Delirious and passed some guitars to them for missions. Martin Smith has always shown an interest in what we are doing with Guitar Aid. He was one of the first to endorse our vision, as early as 2003.

"

Great things start in humble hearts, simple ideas have practical results, and if they are led by God, as for sure Guitar Aid is, the blessing of God is prepared to bear fruit. Your ministry blesses us so much; it brings and encourages. Many good things happen amongst us in Slovakia. Praise God for you!

Marian Lipovsky
Youth for Christ and
Timothy Worship Band

15

Ukraine and Belarus

We have a friend, Sasha, in Ukraine, who spent a couple of years living at Riverside Exeter, and who invited us to take guitars to his country. Sasha said he would organise our programme. Unfortunately, our arrival coincided with the worst snow for 20 years. This would prove to be no problem to Sasha, as he was an expert driving on snow. In spite of flying to Kiev, we still managed to clock up 2,500 miles on that trip.

Driving from Kiev in thick snow was quite an experience. Then we travelled for a few hours to some smaller towns and villages on roads that were barely visible. Our journey to one particular church ended with us having to abandon our vehicle and walk the rest of the way.

I thought of the scripture, "Go into all the world..." This seemed like one of earth's extremities to me, and by far the coldest.

A divine appointment

Our travels took us the length and breadth of the country, from the border of Belarus in the north to Odessa in the south.

We visited one remote church where the pastor called out a young man about 12 years old. As I looked at this lad, I saw so much potential! For two years, he had been praying for his own instrument. Thankfully, we were able to make his dream come true that day. I feel we are surely raising up a new generation of worship leaders that will have an impact on the nations. This scene is repeated in many countries we visit.

As we drove towards Chernihiv, between Kiev and the Belarus border, Sasha asked us, "Shall we follow the ring road around the city, or do you want to drive through the centre?"

Our response was, "Is there a pastor there you know?"

"Yes," he replied.

So we drove to the first petrol station we came to. Sasha phoned his pastor friend, saying where we were and describing the type of car we were in.

"Yes," he replied, "I can see you. I am in the block of flats opposite. I am looking out of my window at your car parked at the garage."

Many times we have meetings like this, which are truly by divine appointment, providing others with the instruments they need.

We went to the pastor's home and his church. We gave his daughter a red electric guitar and his church an electro acoustic. It was heartbreaking when we later watched the news to see the city of Chernihiv being shelled and blocks of flats destroyed in the war. We thought of our timely visit there and prayed for God's protection upon them.

Overcoming disappointment

Liz and I arranged to go to Ukraine together, as I really wanted Liz to experience what I had seen there. We set off for a very early flight. While we were waiting in the early hours of the morning, I must have dozed off, and when I woke I found someone had stolen my bag with the passports. We searched frantically to no avail and had to sit and watch our plane leave without us. We headed back home, feeling dejected and disappointed, and we phoned Sasha to let him know what had happened.

When we arrived home, we were greeted by our daughter Becky, who was very young at the time. "I was praying you would come home," she said. Liz's mum had been staying at our house looking after the children. We could see the funny side of it!

The next day, I contacted our insurance company, who informed us that we were able to claim for everything we had lost. The next job was to replace our passports. Back then, it was possible to go in person to Newport to pick up a passport, so we had the appropriate photos taken, forms filled and we were ready to go. Chris and Ben came with me and thoroughly enjoyed the train ride to Newport. We had a lovely day out.

At that time, I realised that when difficult circumstances come, like someone stealing your passport, how you respond to it can make such a big difference. Through the years, we have learned to trust God when things go wrong. We rebooked our flights, and exactly a week to the day later, set off to Ukraine. Sasha was able to arrange everything to be put back a week.

Adventures in Ukraine

At the first church Liz and I went to in Ukraine, she needed to go to the toilet and was shown to a small cubicle at the bottom of the church garden. Liz was definitely not ready for the sight of a hole in the ground and nothing else. I joked that when I use one, I make the sound of a flush afterwards! I don't think I managed to convince Liz, though.

The locals also insisted we had a traditional sauna. They bought eucalyptus leaves, which were sold on the side of the road. These leaves would be used to hit you gently with as you were in the sauna. That evening, as we got ready for bed, Liz noticed many bruises on my back; either I am too sensitive or they were too enthusiastic in executing the eucalyptus treatment.

On another occasion with John, we went to a church that did violin lessons. The group of young musicians were led by a very austere-looking man, who greatly resembled Lenin, with the same moustache and goatee beard. He sternly looked at us and said, "We know an English song, 'Jinkle Veltz'." They then proceeded to play Jingle Bells at a speed and with an aggression that has left me quivering many times when hearing the song. I joke that I have been left emotionally scarred by his rendering of 'Jinkle Veltz'!

While John and I were there, Sasha took us to a chocolate outlet that sold nice bars of chocolate. I bought enough to include one with every newsletter I sent out with the Ukraine report. "Put the kettle on, have a cup of tea, eat some chocolate while reading the newsletter," was my thinking!

The connection with Sasha was so strong that at one time there was a plan to establish a church there. It is hard to see the destruction that has taken place in Ukraine now, a place we have visited many times. A place of incredible culture and beauty has become a place broken by war. Many of the places we have been to have been badly affected by the constant shelling. The positive thing is that we have had reports of people still using our instruments to worship amid the difficult circumstances.

Belarus and the impact of Chernobyl

On the first of our many trips to Belarus, we realised how much Gomel and the area we were in had been affected by the Chernobyl disaster. Our friend Pastor Dima told us that on the day of the Chernobyl nuclear meltdown, the wind was blowing right in the direction of Gomel. Although Chernobyl is in Ukraine, the consequences of the nuclear radiation were much more severe in neighbouring Belarus. We visited hospitals where, 30 years after the incident, children were still being born with severe respiratory defects due to Chernobyl.

Sitting in a home group in Gomel, the harsh reality of what some people had to endure hit us. Opposite me was a man with a son in his thirties who had severe disabilities. Yes, he had been born not long after the disaster in 1986. For the past thirty-plus years, that family were paying the price of the neglect that led to the reactor exploding.

Our friend Kola told us he went out on his balcony the day after the explosion. He could hardly breathe; the air was thick and felt heavy. He said that he ended up with a bad headache that lasted several days. Kola also told us how he became a Christian. Coming from a strong Roma background, he found it hard to tell his wife when he found the Lord. He kept it quiet for a while. When he kept disappearing, his wife thought he was having an affair, so she and a friend followed him one night. They ended up in an evangelical church, where she heard the gospel and gave her life to Christ. The next week, the pastor spoke on tithing. Kola's wife thought this was a good idea. She went to the front and told the pastor that she had been blessed with a lot of money and wanted to give her tithe. The pastor asked her where she worked and she told him she worked in the market. He then asked her what she sold there. Her reply was, "I don't sell anything; I'm a pickpocket!" The pastor had some explaining to do; this was not the way a Christian should be getting money!

A trip to Moscow

We had always said that Belarus was more Russian than Russia, but now we were about to find out if this were true. Our Ukrainian friend Sasha, who drove us from Kiev to Gomel, told us there was an overnight train we could catch to Moscow. Never wanting to miss the chance of an adventure, John and I readily agreed to go.

The overnight train was quite an experience. We spent most of the time wondering what Russia would be like, what Moscow would be like. One thing Sasha forgot to mention was that to get into Russia you needed a visa. The train doesn't stop at the border of Belarus and Russia, so the visa would be needed on arrival at the train station in central Moscow. We got off the train to be greeted by security police with AK47 rifles at their side. The whole scene was intimidating!

Sasha told us not to worry. He took the officer to one side, had a chat with him and gave him a "20 dollar handshake". Suddenly, the visa didn't seem to matter, and we were free to spend the whole day exploring the city. During the day, we did as much as we could: Red Square, the Kremlin, we saw it all. That night, we caught the train back to Gomel, more aware of how things worked in Russia. When we told Pastor Dima what had happened, we realised things could have been very different. Dima told us that recently a group from Scandinavia had arrived at the same train station with no visas; they were arrested and taken to the airport and deported!

We returned many times to Pastor Dima and the church in Gomel. Each time we went, we would take as many guitars as we could and shared the word the Lord had given us in Pentecostal, charismatic, Roma and Orthodox churches alike. When we went back to Kiev, we made a point of visiting the museum of the Chernobyl disaster. We saw mutations in animals that I would not like to describe! The consequences of Chernobyl really marked the start of the fall of Communism, three years before the Berlin wall came down and Romania and the whole of Eastern Europe opened up.

Take the Next Step

When I was 12, I started to play the keyboard in the worship team. At 19, I felt God call me to service as a worship leader. One of my dreams was to have my own personal guitar. I saw on Facebook that Guitar Aid organisation gives guitars to worship leaders. I sent a message thinking I would not get a reply, but the feedback was positive and a guitar was sent to me. I was really shocked and grateful to God. I am very pleased with the guitar I got; it sounds great and it's just perfect! I love what you do, Guitar Aid; thank you very much for your generosity and love at work. This wonderful gift has inspired me to make new music, new songs that worship God. Be blessed in your service, and thank you very much; may the blessing of God be on you and your sponsors.

Avdija Jasarevic
Worship Leader
Vranje, Serbia

Take the Next Step

16

Revisiting Asia

I have always had a great relationship with AOG. I was once contacted by Roy David, the founder of World Christian Ministries, to say he had proposed to the West Country AOG that they should adopt Guitar Aid as their designated charity for the year. As a result of his efforts and enthusiasm, the region raised over £4,000 for our work.

Roy David had been on many missions throughout his life and had many global contacts. After the support he had given, it seemed natural to ask him where he though the need was for our guitars. His answer? "India."

So John and I started to plan to go to India. I remember packing up the box of guitars we were taking with us to India and thinking, "I could squeeze one more guitar in the box," making a total of seven guitars.

First time in India

We went to Bangalore to be greeted by Pastor Minova Nickelson, who placed garlands of flowers round our neck. The smell and coolness of the flowers were so refreshing amidst the heat of Bangalore. The process of being draped with garlands of flowers was repeated on a few more occasions, each time giving relief and refreshment. We drove east for two hours to a town called KGF, which stands for Kolar Gold Fields. At one time, most of the 300,000 people there were dependent on the gold mine for their livelihood. But seven years before our visit, it was closed down. This left an already poor area in a desperate economic situation.

Pastor Minova is responsible for a church of about 600 people, an orphanage of 110 children and a Bible College of 50 students training to be pastors. A few years before our visit, Minova had been given a guitar, only to have it taken from him, as in his culture his older brother had to have it. Someone said to him, "God will give you seven times what you lost." Here we were years later, bringing a box of seven guitars, fulfilling the prophecy given to him. At that moment, I remembered squeezing in the extra guitar!

The children from the orphanage put on a special show for us. This included singing gospel songs, dance and mime. They performed as if to an audience of hundreds; what a privilege to be there! After the performance, they all lined up to receive sweets that we had bought in the market. Such a small gift, but received with so much appreciation, too.

The guitars were greatly appreciated. We preached and sang to packed-out churches wherever we went. At the churches, there was an absence of cars as everyone came to church on a bike; the sight of so many bikes outside a church was new for us!

I would love to return to India and take more guitars there. We have a great relationship with Philippa Hanna, the well-known Christian recording artist. Whenever she goes on missions, we have told her she can take guitars from Guitar Aid. On one of her trips to India, she took a lovely white Tanglewood electro acoustic. She used it herself while there, then gave it away before she left.

Vietnam and the Philippines

Andy David, who runs World of Worth along with his wife Rachel, used to be in my youth group at Exeter AOG. He invited John and me to go on a mission with him to Vietnam and the Philippines. This proved to be quite an adventure.

We arrived in Hanoi to meet up with a team from Lancashire, headed up by Bobby Ball's daughter. They had gone there to renovate an orphanage. We joined them and spent a fruitful day painting flowers, butterflies and other things on the walls to cheer up the orphanage.

On the Sunday, we met at the music school; this was a front for the Christians to be able to meet in secret. Our arriving at the music school with guitars didn't seem at all suspicious to the authorities, which was a good thing. The lady who interpreted for us had paid dearly for her faith, having been arrested many times and put in prison and receiving beatings on several occasions. It made us aware of how much freedom we have in the West.

The hypocrisy of Vietnam hit us as we had breakfast in the hotel. The local Madame walked through, followed by an entourage of young girls, off to do their work with any Westerner willing to pay the fee. How could worshipping God be forced underground, yet such a public display of immorality be accepted? This is Vietnam!

Having read about it, we were keen to find the prison the American soldiers called the 'Hanoi Hilton'. We found it, along with pictures of one of its most famous residents, John McCain, the Republican nominee for presidency in 2008 and prominent politician. I have to say that the display, along with the videos being shown, was nothing short of Communist propaganda. We moved on from Vietnam to the Philippines.

Sipaway Island

One of the most remote places I have ever been to is Sipaway Island. We flew from Manila to Ilu Ilu and stayed the night there with missionaries. The next day, we caught the ferry from Ilu Ilu to Negros. We had to drive from one side of Negros to the other, over a range of mountains. As we got into the outrigger to travel the final leg of the journey, we knew this was going to be quite different. They informed us we were the first Westerners for over 50 years to stay overnight on the island. One thing I remember about the place we stayed at was the Coca Cola was warm, as was the coffee! Nothing was properly hot or cold!

We visited a school on the island, where the gift of a guitar was received with much enthusiasm; then on to a little church packed out with people to give another guitar. The scenery on this island was breathtaking. The sunset was magnificent; it felt like we were in paradise. In the morning, Andy and I opted to go for a swim in the beautiful turquoise water. This was a moment in time I will never forget. Such natural beauty, yet poverty was rife.

We set off on the long journey to Ilu Ilu. That evening, we were to take a meeting in an outreach church in the slum area of the city. The conditions there were squalid and filthy; rickety walkways above and the stench of stagnant water beneath. People lived in nothing more than tin shacks, yet in that environment I could hear the sound of someone setting up my guitar for the worship time. Hearing a Guitar Aid instrument whilst in despicable circumstances strengthened my resolve to give more. I reflected on the sunrise I had seen on the paradise island, and here I was seeing the sunset in the worst slums I have ever witnessed. This is a country of contrasts. Times like this make me glad I have been called to give instruments of worship to those that need them; raising a voice of praise in a place that seems to have no hope. This will bring the love of Jesus to those who don't feel loved.

Cornerstone and Sefton Village

In the north of the country, we went to Sefton Village, where we met the Scottish missionaries Mark Richie and his wife. Having lived in Scotland for ten years, John and I immediately bonded with them. The work going on there is extensive: street pastors, feeding programme, prison ministry, hospital visitation, it's all going on there. When we visited the prison, we could hardly believe the size of the cells and how many were crammed in. What an atmosphere there was in that prison, with so many inmates having given their lives to Jesus. The time of worship we had with them seemed to just flow naturally as the Spirit of God moved in that place. The hospital visits were special as well. It's the only place I have been where you can freely pray for the patients even though they are no relation to you.

What is being achieved in the Philippines by the Christian community is massive. It was a privilege to take guitars to so many churches there and be involved in their programmes. I met a lady in the market while on duty with street pastors there; she hadn't been to church for several years. I told her God still loved her and wanted to be in her life again. Right there and then, she decided to recommit her life back to God.

The scariest thing on the trip was when we went to sample the expertise of the local barber, who gave us a very close shave! Andy threatened to have John's moustache shaved off. Realising this would be a sin of enormous proportion, Andy backed down and the moustache stayed!

"

Thank you, Guitar Aid and Philippa, for this beautiful guitar. The best part is, I was praying for a Tanglewood guitar and I got the same. I'm enjoying playing it for Jesus. Thank you again! God bless you!

Rajiv Vijiyan
Worship leader
Mumbai, India

17

The greatest need

"Where in the world do they need our help the most?"

We were introduced to missions in 1990 through John Wildriane, so it seemed quite natural to ask him this question now, 16 years later.

"Burkina Faso in West Africa," was his reply without any hesitation.

We often hear people say they would go anywhere in the world for the Lord, but it's quite different asking the likes of John Wildriane where in the world should we go. I can't think of anyone with more worldwide contacts than him!

Burkina Faso

Having already sent some guitars to Burkina Faso previously, we knew they would appreciate what we had brought. Before we left, we had made an agreement with the airline that we could take 12 guitars without incurring any excess baggage charge.

One time back home, Liz and I had been asked if we could accommodate a couple of students from the IBTI for a couple of months. One of the students was Aurel from Romania, the other was Benjamin from Burkina Faso. Because we have a Benjamin in our family, our new guest was affectionately known as 'Big Benjamin'. I was looking forward to seeing Big Benjamin again.

As soon as we arrived, we realised this place was like no other that we had been to before. Without doubt, it is the poorest nation we have visited. They told us how five years ago a war had badly affected them, then two years ago a famine had hit them hard, leaving many suffering and surviving on next to nothing. What a blessing to go to the villages and see wells that have been sponsored by AOG GB. We met up with 'Big Benjamin', who had stayed in our home and shared memories of our time together in Exeter.

It was decided, at the end of our visit, that the guitars would be given to the pastors of the churches and Bible Colleges that we had visited. We found it humbling to sit in a room with these men, who told us stories of how they had triumphed over adversity. We were presented with a leather map of Africa to commemorate our visit. What they lack materially, they more than make up for spiritually. The churches are full, vibrant and buzzing with an air of excitement rarely experienced anywhere else. The main focus of the church's outreach is building schools. We were impressed with the way the pastors have been determined to make up for what the government has lacked in educational support.

We met a guitarist, Augustine. He was proud to be able to give us a CD that he had recorded using a guitar that we had previously sent out to him. He was probably the best guitarist we met on the trip. In fact, we were pleasantly surprised by the standard of musicians. The young people were keen to pick up any tips we could give them. Life is harder in Burkina Faso than anywhere else we had visited, and they always pray for rain, as often the riverbed is dry.

We are more at home in smaller churches where it is possible to meet and chat with the leaders and the youth. The congregations in Burkina Faso were so big and with so many churches to visit, we were often taken to a church, ushered on to the platform to preach or give a greeting, then whisked off to the next church, without even having a chance to connect with anyone. But that was how it was. John and I both had to agree that the needs in Burkina definitely justified John Wildriane's comment that they needed our ministry the most. Confident that all the guitars we had taken would be well used, we headed home.

Reflecting on the trip, we decided to give a full update to John Wildriane. While doing so, we asked, "Where should we go next John?"

His reply came back, again without hesitation. "Togo."

We thank God for men like John who trust us with their contacts in other countries and willingly send us on their behalf.

Togo

Just 25 years before we visited Togo, there had only been a handful of churches there. The church growth that was now being experienced was incredible. Each new church needed a pastor, a worship leader and, subsequently, musical instruments. In Africa, it's easier to start off with a guitar, because it's so portable and has all the elements needed: rhythm, melody and harmony.

We were thrilled to meet up with some of the pastors from Togo. At the time of our visit, they had over 1,000 churches and about 500 pastors. 80% of the population have no formal education, which is in stark contrast to their neighbour Ghana, where smartly dressed schoolchildren laugh and play in the sun. Sunday services start at 7 am and often go on long into the afternoon. Togo has little or no opportunity for tourism or for foreign visitors. It was wonderful to have a glimpse into their world.

The instruments we took would be impossible to obtain, as there was not a single music shop to be found on our visit. They were delighted with the guitars we brought. I didn't realise what an impact our instruments would have until I visited Togo again, 12 years later, which I will tell you about in due course.

Ghana

We crossed the border to visit Janet Wheeler, a missionary to Ghana from Exeter. We noticed a big contrast in Africa between countries that had been controlled by the British and those that were predominantly French. We were proud that the British heritage concentrated on schools, roads, hospitals and government. Many of the more resourceful people in Lome, the capital of Togo, sent their children to school just across the border to Ghana.

Moldova, the poorest country in Europe

We have a friend in Exeter, Hugh Scudder, who is director of a charity that has the plight of the people in Moldova at the core of its operations. Hugh put us in touch with Johan Ribka, his contact in Moldova. We planned to visit the next time we went to Romania.

We had already driven over 1,500 miles to get to Romania when we took the overnight train to Iasi. We sat in the train compartment, unaware of what the sleeping arrangements would be on a night train. At the appointed time, the seats were turned into a flat platform that took the form of a bed. You had to 'top and tail' with whoever was opposite you in the carriage. I was opposite a very old lady who seemed to have no problem snuggling up to me. Thankfully, we stayed fully dressed, apart from kicking off our shoes so as not to hit anyone. Once in Iasi, we got a minibus to take us along with the guitars to Chisinau, where we were glad to be met by Johan Ribka. Somehow, after all that travel – the drive to Romania, the train to Iasi, the minibus to Moldova – it seemed a long, long way from home!

Moldova was so much poorer than anywhere we had been in Romania. The Soviet Communist influence was so much stronger. We went to Transnistria, which is still part of Russia. It was a surreal experience, seeing the guards in Russian uniform with AK47s by their side. We found the whole experience quite intimidating and felt a sense of relief when we finally left, arriving back on Moldovan soil.

We were taken to the site of a women's prison. We were not allowed in, but looking in from fields above the complex, we could see how harsh an environment it was. During the entire time we were in Moldova, we could feel the sense of oppression the country was under. We are in awe of the ongoing, tireless work that Hugh Scudder had committed to and the impact he is having on so many poor families. We often send guitars for Hugh to take to Moldova. Worship has such a positive impact on places like this where life can be so hard.

Meeting the needs

I see Guitar Aid as the middleman between those needing a guitar and the people that have caught the vision of supplying instruments of worship around the globe. The monthly sponsors are the lifeblood and the very foundation that Guitar Aid's success has been built on.

I try to get photos of recipients whenever possible. Each of these photos will go to a sponsor. These photos are sent along with our newsletter. Many tell me how much it means to them to see someone with a guitar they have sponsored. Only eternity will tell the impact being given a guitar for worship will have on those that receive them.

I know that each and every one of our supporters feels involved and part of the giving process. Giving a guitar is a practical gift, with spiritual fruit.

Talent and enthusiasm but no instrument to play, overflowing hearts but
empty hands – this is normal for a vast
number of young, aspiring worship
musicians, and I have witnessed it
time and time again.

Guitar Aid has been addressing this
need for 25 years now, by providing
instruments to those who never
thought it possible to afford them. If
you are grateful for having an instrument in your hands, why not give
thanks in a practical way, by helping to
put one in a pair of empty ones!

Graham Kendrick

Take the Next Step

18

Special occasions

One significant moment for Guitar Aid was when we gave the 3,000th guitar at Campfest in Slovakia. As John and I handed over the guitar, we were not prepared for what was to come. In front of the 7,000 worshippers, the main stage started to fill up with individuals who had received guitars from us and those that had been impacted by our vision. We were both handed T-shirts with the verse 1 Chronicles 23:5: "And four thousand will praise the Lord with instruments I have made." This verse makes reference to the fact that King David had given four thousand instruments. What an example he is, what an honour to be involved in giving instruments of worship!

Learning young

Having our own Land Rover and trailer gave us the luxury of organising trips whenever we wanted. It also gave us the opportunity to take whoever we wanted with us. For me, one of my priorities was to take my children one at a time to experience what was happening all across Europe. I had no problem getting permission from the schools, as they saw the journey as a great geography field trip. When one of my children came with me, I set them the task of producing a project of the journey. For each country we visited, they had to enter into a prepared sheet the towns and cities we went through, the flag and the currency. This was before the euro, so each country had different coins they could collect. Each country had three headings: Food, Culture and Transport. As well as writing on these categories, they also collected things that were specific to the country. By the end of a trip, nine countries had been visited and a project produced that was greatly admired by the teachers when they got home.

One time, we were having difficulty getting through the Hungarian border. When we presented the documents for customs, they looked at one piece of paper and said, "It's not original." We sat there for what seemed an age, trying to convince them that it was genuine, but to no avail. Chris had a Toblerone bar he had been keeping to eat when he got to Romania. John asked Chris if he could have the chocolate, and since Chris was fed up waiting, he was happy to oblige. John took the Toblerone and handed it along with the paper they had rejected. "Ah, I see it *is* original," was the reaction of the border guard. Much to Chris' amusement, we were able to travel on as a result of him giving his chocolate.

The biggest surprise for Chris on this trip was that, being just ten years old, he witnessed children the same age as him, and younger, homeless, drunk and smoking down by the railway station. The thought that they had been abandoned by their parents was difficult enough for us to comprehend, even more difficult for someone as young as Chris.

On another occasion, we were entering Romania late at night and Dan was with us. He was asleep when we went through border control and wasn't noticed by the border guard. After we had completed our mission to Romania, we set off for home. At the border, they said we had an extra child with us, as Dan hadn't been counted on the way in. They were convinced we were smugglers and Dan was a Romanian orphan we were trying to get out. When questioned, Dan only mumbled, adding to the suspicion of the officials. We tried our best to get Dan to speak, but still all he would mutter was a mumble. It was starting to get serious now; the border guards were not amused and we were heading for trouble. We had to shout at Dan, to which he responded, "Why are you shouting at me? I'm tired and I want to go to sleep." At this point, they realised he was English and agreed to stamp our passports and let us leave.

Now they are grown up, our children often speak with affection of the times they went on an Eastern European tour in the Land Rover. One of the lovely things that happened was, when we arrived at the orphanage, our children met with children from Romania and the language barrier disappeared as they played joyfully together. They still treasure the projects that they completed on those fabulous adventures. The countries visited included France, Belgium, Germany, Austria,

Hungary, Poland, Czech Republic, Romania, Slovakia and Croatia. Some geography field trip!

Csilla in Serbia

Having given over 4,000 guitars to date, there are some moments that stick out more than others, like the story of the boy raised by monkeys. Sometimes we are not there to see the reaction of someone receiving. I will let Csilla tell her story of the time she received a guitar from us.

"My name is Csilla. I am 13 and live in Serbia. I came from a Christian family and I follow the Lord. A while ago, the thought entered my mind that I would like to learn to play the bass guitar. In January 2013, we started to pray for an instrument. In the meantime, I started to really walk with Jesus, to have a closer relationship with him. Sometimes I asked God if I would ever receive the guitar, but every time I asked, it was as if he answered, "Pray for it more." So I continued to pray.

"In September, Pastor Viktor called me and said that he had heard about my prayer request and promised me that he would try to help me get a guitar. One month later, my dad said to me that he would take me to a church service in another church where guests from England would speak about worship. The service was excellent. At the close of the meeting, the guests started to hand out acoustic guitars to visitors from other churches.

"At last, my name was called. As I stood up and went to the front, I felt very strange and I didn't understand the whole deal. But I quickly saw that the guitar case I was to get looked totally different from the rest. Then they took it out of the case and it was a Ferrari red bass. My jaw dropped. I couldn't say anything. I wanted to laugh and cry at the same moment. That moment was indescribable. Suddenly, I understood that it was worth it to pray so much, and I knew that it was God who answered my prayer.

"In the evening, when I got home and showed the guitar to my siblings, my sister was so happy for me, and my little brother started to weep because he saw that Jesus really takes care of us.

"Thank you all for this bass guitar! God bless you!"

Csilla's dad is a keen photographer. He captured an iconic image of Csilla jumping into the air with her bass guitar. The picture oozes excitement! I used this picture to advertise our 25th anniversary celebration. We will never forget the reaction of giving that guitar.

The lost is found

I had a surprise invitation to John Hornby Skewes HQ in Leeds. The year 2010 marked 20 years of Guitar Aid and JHS working together. To honour this relationship, I was presented with a fabulous white guitar, with oriental mother-of-pearl inlays adorning the whole length of the neck. Mr Skewes himself handed the guitar to me. The photographer was at the ready, capturing the moment. In due course, many of the guitar magazines carried a feature on 20 years of giving guitars. I was delighted to receive this instrument and hung it up in the Guitar Aid room at Riverside Church. About a year after the presentation, I went into the room where I kept the guitar to find it gone! I could hardly believe it, but sure enough, the guitar was gone.

Jesus tells the story of the joy that is experienced when something that was lost is found: the lost sheep, one out of a hundred; the lost coin, one out of ten; the lost son, one of two sons. The greater the value, the greater the loss. The lost guitar…

For about two to three years, the guitar was missing. Then one day, a friend called me. "I have seen one of your guitars for sale on Gumtree; something doesn't seem right." Sure enough, there it was, in all its glory for anyone to see. It was being sold in Teignmouth, 13 miles away from Exeter.

I rang up to find that it had been sold to a second-hand shop that had quite a few musical instruments. I explained the history of the guitar and my desire to get it back. I gave the shop owner two options: I could ring the police and let them deal with the situation, or he could tell me how much he paid for it and I would cover his cost. He was glad to accept the latter solution. For £90, I redeemed back a guitar that was rightfully mine.

It is incredible how it came back with not a mark on it years after it was taken. I guess I will never know who took it, but that doesn't matter. The guitar that was lost had been found. It now has pride of place on the wall of my dining room.

Guitar Aid celebrations

The relationship between Guitar Aid and the leadership of Riverside Church has always been excellent. Each year, Guitar Aid can have one Sunday to promote the vision and thank the supporters. Over the years, we have had some amazing events. One thing is for sure: the church will always be packed out on one of these evenings. Over time, we have built up a base of faithful supporters who share the vision to raise up new musicians and new worshippers. Inviting the supporters to a Guitar Aid celebration is a way of saying thank you to them. Liz and her team have perfected the art of providing a buffet at the end of the evening. Paul and Rose, our connect group leaders, have a gift for hospitality. Their job is to look after the visiting band and their team. I must say, they look after our guests as if they were royalty!

The first event we had was a Bryn Haworth concert. It was after this event that Bryn gave me his Black Ovation Custom Legend, which I passed on to Marian in Slovakia.

The evening with Chaos Curb and Dave Griffiths was memorable. That evening we were celebrating 25 years of Guitar Aid. At one point, Dave stopped playing, looked up and said, "Don't tell me there haven't been sacrifices along the way." That comment really touched me, and yes, there have been sacrifices, but the rewards of service by far outweigh the cost.

Slovakia has featured greatly in our Guitar Aid Celebrations. Miro Toth came one year and gave us some valuable lessons on how to bring a standard of excellence to all we do. Brano Letko and his family came. What a weekend that was – the worship was simply off the scale! Everyone at Riverside warmed to his anointed, sensitive style of worship. Marian has featured a few times, but the most recent was the best.

John and I were in Slovakia and staying at Marian's house. Marian took us over to Mino's house to see where he practices his drums. With Marian and Mino together, I popped the question to both of them.

"Would you like to bring Timothy Worship Band to the UK for a Guitar Aid celebration? We will cover all your costs."

Their reaction was priceless. "Wow, yeah!" shouted Mino. "We are going to England!"

So it was agreed the whole band and sound engineer would come over to the UK for the next event. We have a lovely sister in our church,

Christine Janaway, who has a guest house. Chris agreed to have the whole band at a special rate. It was absolutely brilliant to have the whole band staying together at her home.

The Sunday morning worship was incredible; people just couldn't wait for the evening event. As the doors opened that evening, the sense of anticipation was building. To this day, I still hear people talking about that worship event. Marian, Mino and the Timothy Worship Band are definitely firm favourites at Riverside.

For me, I love saying thank you to our supporters, and a Guitar Aid celebration evening is the perfect way to do it.

Riverside mission to Poland, Czechia and Slovakia

Years later, we received an invitation to take the Riverside Church band to Campfest, and we started to plan the trip. The sight of the official poster with 'Riverside Worship Band' in print added to the excitement. We had a few Polish families in our church, so the plan was that we would fly to Poland and have fellowship at the home church in Lubin, the church of one of the families now living in Exeter. They would organise the hire of a coach to take us on to Slovakia.

We ended up with 22 of us in total. When we arrived, we had wonderful fellowship with our newfound Polish friends. We led the worship and preached in their church. They also organised a barbecue for us to enjoy with them. Our next stop was Czech Republic to meet with Pastor Lubo, who John and I had met in Albania.

It was decided that we would stop off at Auschwitz on the way. This is an experience none of us will forget. The mood on the coach after was silent and sombre. As we pulled up to Lubo's youth event, we were mobbed by excited, enthusiastic young people that wanted to play games with us. This was the perfect antidote to the mood we were in after Auschwitz. We had a wonderful evening with them.

We all stayed in the basement of the church in Český Těšín, where John and I had visited many times. The next day, we set off for Slovakia and Campfest.

Driving through the beautiful valley in Slovakia, with the river flowing alongside, I realised that no one else on the bus had been to Slovakia, not even the driver. It was wonderful to feel that I would be able to introduce my church in Exeter to my friends there. The emotion of it brought tears to my eyes.

It was great to play at Campfest three times at different venues, but the highlight for me was seeing a special guitar being used. Bryn Haworth had given me a black Ovation Custom Legend. To buy one of these new would cost over £2,000. I had felt I should give this guitar to Marian. He had then used it for a few years at concerts and on albums, after which he had felt he should pass it on to a young worship leader, Julius Slovak. When I saw Julius leading worship with over 5,000 people there, I felt a fire burn inside me.

I could feel the tears rolling down my cheeks as I sensed the Lord speaking to me: "Whatever you have given, give more; however fast you have run with this vision, run faster; however good the guitars have been, give better."

I was seeing firsthand the fruit of years of giving instruments, some of which had then been faithfully passed on. This was a very special time for me. *Slovakia* had become a very special place.

Take the Next Step

The prophet Habakkuk spoke a promise that "the earth will be filled with the knowledge of the glory of the Lord as the waters cover the sea" (Hab.2:14). What David Sumner does through Guitar Aid is to work tirelessly to release this promise. By equipping worship leaders around the world with quality instruments, Guitar Aid is practically and lovingly releasing the sound of heaven, the sound of glory, across the earth. What a promise, what a vision!

Dave Griffiths
Chaos Curb

19

Africa revisited

From time to time, God puts a place on our hearts and we feel compelled to go there. Such was the case with Uganda. Having had a successful trip to Vietnam and the Philippines with Andy David, we asked him about his contacts in Uganda. He was quick to point out to us that if you were going to Uganda, then you must also visit Ethiopia. It happened that his contact from Ethiopia would be in Torquay the next week. I was delighted to be able to meet up with Bishop Teklu, the head of the churches in Ethiopia. So the mission was planned.

Uganda

Arriving in Uganda was very special. We remember the raid on Entebbe airport and the history involved with it. We were greeted by Bishop Isaac, who heads up the churches in Uganda. Isaac is responsible for overseeing 1,235 churches in 13 regions of Uganda. We headed north for a three-hour drive to Masindi. The church leaders had complained to him that they never get any foreign visitors to that area. The day after this request, Andy David contacted him, telling him of our desire to go to Uganda.

When we arrived at Masindi, the road to the church was lined on both sides with people cheering our arrival. Wow! We felt like royalty. We arrived to be told we were taking a three-day crusade that had been organised by 13 pastors and their churches. What a celebration it was! Hundreds gathered in a tin hut; that was their church. No lights, no electricity, no windows. What had we come to? But these people were hungry for God. The sessions started at 10 am and went on until it was too dark to continue. The church was surrounded by mud huts. At

167

lunchtime, we enjoyed a meal that had been prepared over an open fire. Amid these humble surroundings we found a people that were full of the Holy Spirit with a passion for Jesus that was infectious.

Ethiopia

After the wonderful time in Uganda, we flew on to Ethiopia. Our first experience there was not a good one. We arrived at the airport at 6 pm, expecting no problems, as in so many countries we visit. However, the customs officials on duty were determined to make our lives as difficult as possible for us. During the long delay, we could see Teklu waiting for us on the other side of the customs gate. The officials demanded $300 duty for the guitars, but Teklu said we should not pay it. They sent us to one desk, then another, all to no avail. Eventually, six hours later, a different shift came on to work and we finally entered Ethiopia, having paid just $90 duty on the guitars. Ethiopia is one of the poorest countries we have visited. In spite of the poverty, they just keep smiling and giving everything to Jesus.

What an incredible experience, travelling for hours to get to our destinations. In most cases, the last 20 minutes of the journey was over fields, passing by remote villages, to even more remote churches. In these churches, the service happened at whatever time you arrived there. It was humbling to find that 50 or more people had assembled at church waiting for our arrival.

The Bishop told us how much the people had sacrificed for their faith in God. Both in Ethiopia and Uganda, they said we were the first people from England to visit the church. It is hard to imagine such remote places when we live in such a modern culture, with instant communication at our fingertips.

There are few places we have been that needed the guitars as much as Ethiopia. Jihad, our guide in that area, told us that when he had become a Christian, his family had disowned him, because he had brought shame to them. His wife was given to his brother. We found it hard to imagine how much Jihad had sacrificed to be a Christian. It was an honour to meet him and listen to his story.

On the way to the village where we chatted with Jihad, we saw that a cow had been killed by traffic. Villagers were making the most of this, taking large chunks of meat from the animal. On our return, it was a different story; a pack of dogs were savaging the animal, blood covering their faces. Just out of reach of the dogs, there must have been dozens of vultures waiting for their turn. This sight made us realise how difficult things were in this part of the world – the food chain from humans to vultures!

Egypt mission

Going to the missions conference in Bromley was the start of a new path for me, because God has opened up new opportunities, like when Ron Hibbert invited me to Egypt at the conference.

Ron was the only person I knew on that trip. We all met up at Heathrow Airport. I arrived before Ron and was greeted by a group of AOG pastors. Paddy Venner, the pastor of Eternity Church Norwich, said to me, "You must be Dave… Ron likes you… and if Ron doesn't like you, he will tell you!" That made me laugh, but also made me feel accepted by these great guys. We enjoyed great fellowship on that trip, and I shared a room with Pastor Phil Pye.

We arrived in Egypt at a time when the Christians had experienced significant persecution. Their response to this was love and forgiveness. Egypt is strategically placed and has a significant impact on the surrounding countries. We heard how much persecution and suffering was being experienced by many of the surrounding nations. We are blessed to be able to practically encourage Christians in these circumstances.

Our guitars not only went to Egypt but also to missionaries from Yemen and Algeria. During our time in Egypt, we were able to have a live link with missionaries in the Yemen. It's hard to imagine life there with a war raging around you. When we visit Africa, John and I often fly to Libya, spending time in Tripoli airport. It brought home to me the sense of destruction, as we saw pictures of the total devastation of that airport.

The missions team at Egypt dramatically recreated an area in the grounds of where we were staying, depicting scenes from the surrounding countries. It was deeply touching to hear these stories firsthand. In Cairo, we visited the cave church, where as many as 20,000 meet for all-night prayer meetings. Worshipping with these believers was very special.

Returning to Egypt

The first trip anywhere is always the most important. When you go to a new country, you have the opportunity to check the spiritual temperature of the nation. There are many other things, both cultural and spiritual, that can only be experienced firsthand. There is something special about telling people, "We will be back," and then fulfilling that promise with a second visit. The second visit to Egypt was headed up by the capable hands of Simon Jarvis, along with a group of pastors from the UK. I enjoyed the fellowship of sharing a room with Gowan Wheeler, the son of Janet Wheeler, Exeter AOG's missionary to Ghana.

The purpose of the trip was to encourage young people from more rural parts of Egypt. Around 200 young people were brought together for a three-day event. The atmosphere during our time together was incredible. The theme of the event was 'who you are in God', and the key teaching was, "What you do matters.... Who you are matters more." So the young people embarked on a journey of discovering who they were in God.

Simon asked me, "What are you going to do with the guitars?" About 20 different churches were represented, so I thought it would be a good idea for each church to write the reason why they should have a guitar. Simon loved the idea. The notes from each church were given to the Egyptian leadership, who sorted through them and chose the ones to receive a guitar. I was really impressed with how delighted they all were to see the guitars given. Even churches that didn't get one seemed overjoyed for the ones that did. I was witnessing a true Christlike spirit in these young Egyptian Christians. It was unforgettable.

Being an engineer and a toolmaker, I always appreciate the technical aspects of anything made of metal. To stand and look at Tutankhamun's gold mask, created in 1323 BC, had me completely captivated. I looked at the detail, the craftsmanship, the symmetry. I just looked in wonder and complete awe at the skill that had gone into making such a beautiful mask.

I made many friends in Egypt and am grateful to Ron Hibbert for sharing his passion for this nation with me. As well as collecting a flag from each nation I visit, I also like to collect Starbucks mugs. Whenever I drink out of my Egypt mug, memories come flooding back.

King David was the first one to hire musicians and singers full-time, to have 24/7 worship going on in his tent (continuous fire on the altar). He understood the importance of praise and also the importance of the musical instrument. I believe Guitar Aid are aware of these two important aspects; this is why they help, providing many worship leaders around the globe with free, quality guitars.

Philip Wissa
Arabic worship leader
Egypt

Take the Next Step

20

A Macedonian call

At the request of Pastor Aran, I was invited to attend a mission's conference at Bromley. I went up with Andy David, who was part of the National Missions team. We arrived early and went for a wander around the town. As I was walking through the centre of Bromley, I clearly heard in my spirit God say, "A new door is opening."

I took some guitars with me that were handed out to the visiting missionaries that were at the event. I met Mark Wiltshire, who was heading up the missions team. I had given him guitars before, but this was the first time meeting in person. As a result of that meeting, I was invited to go on the mission to Egypt with Ron Hibbert, who has been the pioneer of missions in AOG for many years. It was decided they would have another mission's conference in Macedonia, and I was also invited to that. I met Lyubo Petkov from Bulgaria, who asked if I would visit his church after the conference in Macedonia. So many invites, so many new contacts made... For sure God was opening a new door for me.

Associate missionary

During the trip to Egypt, Ron had told me that I should be an associate missionary with AOG. Mark agreed.

I had never thought of having a position; I was more concerned about functioning and being faithful to my vision of giving guitars for worship. However, Ron had planted a seed that would bear much fruit in the future. This was the start of a wonderful journey, following in my father's footsteps.

Wherever we go, people ask us about Ron. He, along with John Wildreane from the IBTI Bible College, pioneered the whole concept of short-term missions. Aurel, who was the first person I ever met on missions in 1990, told us that when he was a little boy in 1962, he remembers Ron and John visiting his family in Romania. I have the greatest of respect for both these men of God and their vision, and their ability to see the vision through.

Macedonia missions conference

The purpose of the mission in Macedonia was to get all the pastors and leaders in the Balkans together. Having travelled extensively around the Balkans with John in the Land Rover, I was really excited at what could happen at this event. I had brought six guitars to give away and thought that would be my duty complete. Ron had different ideas.

On the way to the place we were staying at, we stopped off for a drink. Ron came up to me and said, "When we get there, come and see me, as I want you to help me by looking after the finance of the trip."

I was shocked. I could so easily have said that I don't do finance, I do guitars, but something inside me said, "Servant heart, Dave."

I met Ron as requested, and he detailed my assignment. They needed to know how many cups of coffee we were all going to drink, how many meals we would have, how far each of the delegates had travelled, how much we needed to give them to cover travel expenses, the list went on. I learned an important lesson; I had moved completely out of my comfort zone, yet I knew that everything I did in looking after the finances meant that it was something less for Ron to do.

About 30 people attended the conference. I knew many of them; I had been in their homes and shared in their churches. To be part of this meant a lot to me.

Mark Wiltshire was leading the event. He asked if anyone had not had a guitar from me in the past, to which six people raised their hands; those were the ones that received the guitars. David Shearman was one of the guest speakers. It was so good to share time together. My parents were great friends with his.

When the conference finished, I had to go into town to exchange the money to pay for everything. Pastor Venco accompanied me to the bank.

When I handed the receipts for the completed financial transactions to Ron, he said, "Well done! If you hadn't done that, I would have had to do it."

Speaking in Stara Zagora

Next thing, another move out of my comfort zone! I got into a car with Lyubo, who I first met in Bromley, and we drove from Macedonia to Bulgaria, where I was the guest speaker at Lyubo's church in Stara Zagora. I was given a room in the church.

Before the service, I said to God, "It's me and you, Lord." This was the first time I had ever gone to a new country on my own, to a new church with a pastor I had only met once before. That evening, after a wonderful day sharing and serving in the big church, I reflected on the day's events and said to myself, "Me and you, Lord, we didn't do so bad!"

Close call!

One of the hardest things to cope with is when circumstances restrict travel. John was rushed to hospital in 2011 with severe blood loss. They found he had less than half his blood, and he was immediately given five hours of blood transfusions. John said to the doctor that when at home, he had just wanted to go to bed and try to sleep it off. His wife Dorcas and daughter Judith had insisted he went straight to the hospital. "Good job he came in," the doctor said, "as tomorrow he wouldn't have been with us."

After three weeks in hospital and six more blood transfusions, he'd had enough. They were taking blood samples twice a day and having to make three to six attempts each time. He felt so weak, his arms were black and blue, and he just wanted to go home and be with Jesus. The nurse came to take more blood, and he told her nicely to go away and leave him in peace. The doctor then came and told him he must give blood, but he asked her also to leave him in peace. Finally, the consultant came and sat on the bed and explained that there was no choice; this had to happen.

John asked, "If I say no, am I going to die?"

She answered, "Yes, you don't have enough blood to support your organs and very soon they will shut down."

John said he felt ready to meet Jesus and started falling asleep, imagining waking up at the feet of Jesus. Then, at that moment, the room filled with a voice saying, "It is not your time; it is too early."

Something stirred in him. He thought about the woman with the issue of blood and how she had touched the hem of Jesus' garment. Then he thought about Jacob who wrestled with the man of God saying, "I will not go unless you bless me." John took his pillow and held it in a bear hug, and held on to the hem of the blanket, saying, "I will not let go until you bless me." Then he thought of blind Bartimaeus who cried out, "Jesus, son of David, have mercy on me," so John did the same.

He said that suddenly it was like lying on the seashore as wave after wave of God's refreshing river of love and mercy flowed over and through him. He had that assurance that he would be going home to his family.

The doctors found where the blood loss was and operated on him. Two weeks later, John was home.

Travelling with a faithful supporter

The consequences of the time in hospital meant that John was unable to go on missions until he had fully recovered. So I asked my friend Al if he would like to join me on my next mission. Al was going through a period of transition in his business and was delighted to be able to come on the mission with me.

The first stop for us was Macedonia, where we were greeted by my good friend Marino. I had first met Marino 16 years previously, at Osijek Bible College. It was so good for us to have that Macedonian call, "Come over and help us." Much to our surprise, Marino had arranged transport for us for the entire duration of our visit. We travelled the length and breadth of the country, visiting many churches and leaving guitars for their worship groups.

In Kosovo, we met up with Driton, the head of the churches there. This was a great time of fellowship and a time to catch up on what was happening in the Balkans. Driton told us that when John and I had visited him the first time, the guitar they were using had just broken, days before we arrived. He said, "It was like angels coming when you brought us the new guitar!"

One of the highlights of the trip was to be able to go to Albania and meet up with Arnold Geiger again. I met him on our first mission to

Albania in 1992. We have visited many times since, but not in recent years. We were both pleasantly surprised to see how God had led him during the years since we had met.

Al has been one of Guitar Aid's most faithful supporters; it was so good to be enabling him to see the impact we were having firsthand.

Upgrades

Having our own missions vehicle has afforded us the luxury of being able to be flexible about where we go. This has enabled us to go to multiple missions locations with relative ease. How were we going to achieve this without our own vehicle? Wizzair was the answer. We flew into Debrecen, Hungary to be picked up by Pastor Janos.

We were able to take the guitars we needed for the trip on the flight. Being an engineer, I was able to make wheels that could be taped on to the bottom edge of one end of the guitar box. With a handle made of tape at the opposite corner, the box of guitars functioned like a very large case. It could be pulled along with relative ease. I had two sets of these wheels, so 12 guitars could be wheeled along by one person! *Brilliant,* I hear you say! But in all honesty, it saved us a lot of heavy lifting. When I got to the destination, I simply cut the tape off and took the wheels home, ready for next time.

Janos took us to churches in Hungary, where we gave out guitars. He then drove us on to Serbia to our good friend who is now with the Lord, Viktor Sabo. More guitars were given in Subotica. It was Viktor's desire that we travelled the length of Serbia giving guitars. Viktor himself was going to a conference in Macedonia, so the plan was that we would drive with his son-in-law, Atilla, and meet him there. On the way, our fellowship with Atilla was excellent. We had a brilliant time in Nis and other parts of Serbia, connecting with friends from the past, making new friends and, as always, giving guitars.

We eventually arrived in Skopje, Macedonia, where our friend Marino had found a modest hotel for us to stay in. We met up with Viktor, only to find he was staying in a room in the church on a camp bed. John and I went back to our hotel and said, "We can't let our friend Viktor sleep on a camp bed while we are in the comfort of a hotel." So we went to reception and organised for a room for Viktor. I wish you could have seen the delight and relief on his face when we told him he would be staying with us. I honour the memory of Viktor. For many years, he was our point of contact for distribution of guitars in Serbia. He was a good and faithful servant. Viktor was well known by all the church leaders and was respected. John and I are honoured to have been able to call him our friend.

We flew home from Skopje back to Luton Airport, where we had flown out to Hungary ten days before. We had travelled many miles but with so much more ease than taking the Land Rover all the way from Exeter.

One of the benefits of building relationships over the years is that many friends now treat us like family. John and Dorcas have had the privilege of being invited to and attending two weddings in Hungary and two weddings in Romania. Liz and I have also been blessed with experiencing firsthand the cultural difference of a wedding in Romania.

I am very thankful for the guitar I was gifted, especially for the fact that I am left-handed and it is very difficult to find a left-handed guitar. It's hard to believe we have known each other for over 25 years now. I have been blessed personally by Dave's ministry; we have also served on several trips to Bosnia Herzegovina, Albania, Kosovo and Croatia. God has used Guitar Aid worldwide, but for us over here, knowing that there is a ministry dedicated to encouraging the worship of our Lord is extremely important. God bless you and continue to use you in his service.

Pastor Marino Mojtic
Macedonia

Take the Next Step

21

South America

After the missions conference in Stara Zagora, I had sat next to Mark Wiltshire on the flight home. He had also been taking part in the event. We talked about missions and spoke of our mutual desire to go to South America.

"We must do it together sometime," Mark enthused.

True to his word, Mark soon asked me to join him on a mission to South America.

Change of plans

The mission was due to take place directly after the World Pentecostal Conference in Sao Paulo, Brazil. Due to the problem with bird flu, many of the delegates decided to drop out. Mark rang me to tell me there was going to be a change of venue and he would be going at a different time. He and his wife Liz would be celebrating their 25th wedding anniversary, so he decided they would both travel together. I had promised my Liz that I would take her somewhere to celebrate our 30th wedding anniversary, so I told Mark that I wouldn't be able to come.

I remember the call distinctly. We were having a life group meeting when Mark rang.

"Why not bring Liz as well," he suggested, "and by the way, we are going to Peru instead of Brazil!"

In front of our life group, I asked Liz if she would like to go to Peru.

"I can't go to Peru," she answered.

Then, as though with one voice, we all asked, "Why not?"

Liz had no reason for a 'why not', so we agreed to go. Her only concern was how much it was going to cost. I assured her that we were planning a holiday to celebrate our wedding anniversary and the money put aside for that would help towards it.

Flexible and adaptable

Getting to Peru was quite an experience. We packed up a box, holding the absolute maximum number of guitars we could take, and headed off to London to meet up with Mark and Liz.

Sat on the plane, Mark said to me, "Missions must be flexible and adaptable." No sooner had he said this than we were told there was going to be a delay in the flight. We waited and waited... and waited... only to be eventually told that the plane had been damaged and we would all have to get off as the flight was now cancelled. We were put up in the Premier Inn next to the airport and told the airline would pay for us to have a meal.

The evening meal proved to be a wonderful time of fellowship, where Liz and I really got to know and like Mark and Liz. The conversation was mission-based and just naturally flowed as we shared late into the night.

The next day, we boarded the plane. I took particular note of certain features on the old plane to make sure we were on a different one! Arriving in Lima late, we were told we had missed our connecting flight to Cusco. We had to wait as there was no sign of our guitars. When the guitars eventually arrived, the four of us were the only ones left there. The airline decided we should be put up at the five-star Sheraton on Lima, at the expense of the airline. We eventually arrived at Cusco a day later than we originally intended.

Liz needn't have worried about the cost of the trip, because when we eventually got home, we were refunded the full cost of the flights due to the delay. Good old British Airways! We could hardly believe it. Being flexible and adaptable really paid off this time!

Missions conference in Peru

The venue for the meeting was Cusco, Peru. The reason for the conference was to have a personal consultation with missionaries serving in the Americas. It was a time of sharing each other's vision together, but more importantly to let them know that we are thinking about them and praying for them back in the UK. The missionaries were gathered together from Colombia, Panama and various other parts of Peru.

The night before the conference, I walked in the old town of Cusco and Mark asked me if I would do the devotional. That night I didn't sleep. I felt the heavy weight of responsibility of sharing with these wonderful missionaries, who had given up so much for the call of God on their lives.

Mark shared the AOG Missions strategy and how important it was for them not to feel isolated on the mission field. Then it was my turn. I simply shared about how God spoke to Samuel when he was only a boy, but after his time talking with God, he slept, then got up and performed the jobs he had to do in the temple. This was a balance of *vision* and *duty*. For all the great visions we have, there is always some kind of duty to carry out. I finished by showing the embroidery of a Guitar Aid logo with guitar on a T-shirt. The front shows the detail, the back looks a mess, but both are needed. (Later, David Taylor came up to me and encouraged me by saying the message was "spot on". I felt humbled to have had this opportunity.)

Together, we prayed for each other's ministry and had a wonderful time of connecting and encouraging each other. At the end of the time together, we presented them all with guitars to take back home with them.

Spending time in South America was made even more special, as our contact in Cusco, Steve Hobby, had arranged for us to visit many significant places in the Inca heartland. For all of us, the highlight was visiting Machu Picchu. The first view of this amazing place at sunrise takes your breath away. This trip was a wonderful combination of mission and exploration of the country. Mark and his wife Liz celebrated their 25 years of marriage, while Liz and I celebrated our 30 years. This trip enabled us to combine a mission with the unique culture Peru had to offer.

It was on this trip that we first met David Taylor and his wife, Dary. We still stay in touch and we hope to go to Colombia one day, as we have family connections there. My brother-in-law Jon is married to Patty, who was born in Colombia and has family there. One time when they were visiting family in Bucaramanga, I gave them a guitar to give away. They were concerned as to who they should give it to. I told them not to worry and that God would show them. It got to the last couple of days and they still hadn't given the guitar. Patty walked into a shop and God spoke to her to speak to a man in the shop. She asked the man if he needed a guitar and his response was astonishing. He was pastor of a church just a short walk away and they were planning a youth event that evening. They had been praying for a guitar. Wow! Here it was! Patty gave him the guitar. There was great rejoicing in the youth group that night. In gratitude, they gave Patty a leather Bible cover to give to me. It fits perfectly over my Message Bible! I cherish it to this day!

A young worship leader/guitar player arrived at our church, Casa de Oracion, in Colon, Panama, to help us in our ministry. He said to me, "Can you give me a guitar?" I had none to give.

In the mission consultation in Peru, I met David Sumner, who gave guitars to the missionaries. This will help us in our worship and outreach services. Thanks!

Amanda Alvarado
Missionary to Panama

Take the Next Step

22

An era of change

For quite a few years, if you had asked me what the next step was for Guitar Aid, I would have said, "For Guitar Aid to have its own premises." When Buller Road Chapel closed and came up for sale, I found out that the church also had a double garage in a separate location. Gordon Rooke, who knew the trustees, arranged for me to have a look at the premises. Being always the optimist, I could see the possibilities.

I made an offer of £15,000 for the garage. The offer seemed to be fine with the trustees, and the solicitor assured me they would accept my offer. But – and it is a big but – someone came with an offer for the church and refused to complete the purchase unless the garage was included in the deal.

I knew that having our own place was the next step. I felt frustrated that this had fallen through, but Liz said that she had never witnessed that the purchase of the garage was right. Buller Road trustees generously gifted Guitar Aid £5,000 from the sale.

I shared all this with Rose Lille in our church. Rose came from Kenya. She told me not to worry – and that I would laugh when I saw what God was going to do. She was right...

Changes in Eastern Europe

For many years, we had taken aid to Eastern Europe along with the guitars. The only real change in the requirements of the guitars was for better quality instruments. Improving the quality of what we give has

Take the Next Step

been an ongoing process. The situation with the aid had become a different story. We watched as each country in Eastern Europe became more affluent: motorways in Hungary where there used to be small roads; bigger and better shops, and less need for our help. The countries of Eastern Europe were changing. We had to change with them. So instead of taking trailer-loads of general goods, the focus became on specific projects. The need for our own trailer had diminished. Marian from Slovakia had often expressed the desire to get one, so John decided it would be a good idea for us to give our trailer to him for the work of 'Youth for Christ' in Slovakia.

This still left us with our Land Rover. We thought, in spite of the fact that we were both nearly thirty years older than when we had started, it would be good to do one more mission with the Land Rover without the complication of towing the trailer. So the plan was made: we would visit as many of our Eastern European contacts as we could.

First stop was Czech Republic to renew the connection that St Thomas Baptist had with a Baptist church in Liberec. We arrived to find the whole town had been taken over by an international film crew. We were on the set of the new Spiderman movie. To save cost, instead of filming in Prague, they chose the city square of Liberec to make it look as if it were Prague. The extent of the set covered the entire city centre – it was really, really impressive! The fellowship was great, and we met up with people that had come to St Thomas Baptist Church in 1990. They spoke with affection about our wonderful city. We left a couple of guitars with them for their worship group, and we felt like a link from the past had been reconnected. While in Czech, we also managed to catch up with our good friend Jarek, who we first met at IBTI in the early 90s.

All was well as we continued on to Hungary. It was a pleasure to spend time with Janos and revisit a Roma church we had been to 12 years before. What a blessing to see the bass guitar, the electric guitar and the electro/acoustic that we had brought on that visit still being used! When we had gone 12 years earlier, they had had no bass player, but one of the young men had determined to learn. Here he was, years later, proficiently playing with skill and enthusiasm.

Up until now, driving the Land Rover had seemed plain sailing. On to Romania then… We felt sure that our newfound confidence in driving the vehicle would continue for many years, until… *Clunk! Grrr! Clang!* On our way to Arad from Lipova, our gearbox made the most awful noises. We managed to limp into the Harvest Church Arad and, standing

188

in the foyer, phoned our friend Mark. He told us they had a Land Rover mechanic at their church and said, "I will ring him." We then heard a phone ring… Would you believe it, the mechanic was standing next to us and took the call from Mark?!

After careful inspection, we realised it would not be a quick fix as we needed a new gearbox and clutch. Mark agreed to take us on to Serbia while they fixed our vehicle. We went to Subotica to spend what would be our last time with Viktor Sabo. Returning to Romania became a time of frustration, as each day the vehicle repairs would be "finished tomorrow" but quite a few tomorrows came and went. When the vehicle was finally OK, we left Romania five days later than we had originally intended.

John and I felt that God was not just talking to us, but *shouting* that our days of driving thousands of miles from home to the furthest parts of Europe were coming to an end. The many contacts we have made through the years will ensure that we will be able to get around wherever and whenever we need it, so the missions go on!

Fulfilment of God's promise

I was at a crossroads. I had to decide, was I going to retire from secular employment and concentrate on missions and Guitar Aid? I made my mind up and handed in my notice. That evening, I had a call from Mark Wiltshire, who was the AOG Missions Director at that time.

"Would you be willing to join the national missions board to represent the West of England?" he asked.

What an offer! What a confirmation that I was making the right choice.

"Yes, yes!" I replied – a definite yes!

I thought of the first time in Bromley, when I had walked down the high street and heard God say that a new door was opening. This door proved to be a wonderful blessing to me. I have fond memories of my time serving on the AOG Missions board. To meet in a room with such a wealth of experience was incredible. The ever-present Ron Hibbert kept us on our toes!

My mum was particularly delighted at this appointment, and she always said that my dad would have been really pleased that I had become part of this AOG team. I won't ever forget the train rides to

Coventry. I always had to change at New St Birmingham. Being a 'Brummie' herself, my mum loved me to call her when I was there.

On one occasion, I sat next to Leigh Goodwin as he was planning a trip to Togo.

"Are you meeting with Djakouti Mitre?" I asked him.

Leigh was surprised I knew him; Djakouti headed up the whole of the AOG Togo churches. I told Leigh that I had been there with my brother John years before. I was delighted when Leigh asked me if I would like to join him on that trip; I had great respect for him for all the years of dedication he had given to missions. The thought of going on missions together was a sweet thought to me. I am a great believer in travelling in pairs. John and I have saved ourselves a lot of problems by watching each other's backs and working together on missions.

Mum reunited with Dad

From the year 2000 until Mum went to be with the Lord ended up being 18-and-a-half years. I'd made Dad a promise that I would look after her, and I intended to keep that promise. More than anything else, Mum wanted me to spend time with her.

During my last few years working shifts, I would often spend time with Mum. I thank God I took those moments while I could. God clearly gave me the word, "Your times are in my hands." Mum was becoming frail and ready to see Dad again. She spoke significant words into my life. So often she would say when we came back from a mission or when doing something with AOG, "Dad would have been proud of you." I told her that nothing would compensate for losing her. I would often say, "Let's take off our glasses and have a proper hug." During those moments, I would tell her how much I loved her.

One of Mum's favourite sayings was, "We speak the same language." We did, and it was a spiritual one. "I'm only a phone call away," was my motto. I would drop everything to be there. Even a lightbulb being replaced was an emergency! "Where are you now?" was always her first question. She cared about where I was and what I was doing.

I knew I had to take Mum to see Becky and Elias; she so loved that little boy. The last time she had seen Elias, she had taken him off Becky, saying, "I am going to pray for him." She did, and what a powerful prayer it was!

Another time, when I took her to Teignmouth, her favourite place to go, we were like two teenagers, singing 'Leaning on Jesus' at the tops of our voices. There was also a phrase from a song that became special to us: "Sweet will of God, still fold me closer, till I am wholly lost in thee."

Dad and Mum are now together after such a long time. I'm glad she will receive the reward God has for her. It was God's time; who are we to question it? At 93, she had lived a long, fulfilling life. I cherish the words she spoke into my life, and my desire is to carry the mantle of anointing that Dad possessed and the prophet understanding Mum had.

When Mum finally went to be with the Lord, we had to clear things from the house. Finding the train set box that had been given to us as little boys when Dad was in hospital in Harrogate made me cry. I had also promised Mum that if we ever sold the house, I would not sell the garden. John and I came to an amicable agreement about this. We now have a large log cabin on the land, half full of guitars, and a wonderful place to go to remember Mum and Dad. The bonus is, it had become like an allotment and we benefit from the many things we grow there. Mum had a loganberry that stretched along the area of garden we now have. My favourite is Loganberry crumble, using the fruit from Mum's garden.

Back to Togo

It was a privilege to travel with Leigh Goodwin, visiting a country that I had last visited 12 years before, representing AOG GB. Leigh and I were ushered into a room filled with very important-looking people. It was the national AOG leadership team, with representatives from all over Togo. At the head of the table was Djakouti. After all the business was done, Djakouti came to me and said, "On Sunday, you will preach at my church". I was really surprised, but realised that the guitars we had brought years before had been a blessing, and time we had spent connecting with the pastors had paid off.

We attended a graduation ceremony at the Bible College along with a large number of students and their families. The worship was led by keyboard, drums and a bass guitar. To my delight, I found that the guitar was one that John and I had brought on our previous trip. Imagine, for the previous 12 years, that guitar had been used for worship, week in, week out.

Leigh and I had the privilege of travelling to the remote Afeye village with the AOG missionary Philomene Essi. The welcome we received was nothing short of regal. Lined up on both sides of the route were enthusiastic locals cheering and whooping at the tops of their voices. We both had the chance to share in the modest village setting, with a church with open walls. We presented them with a new guitar for their worship team. As you can expect from Africa, the worship was loud, long and enthusiastic, and always accompanied by various forms of dance; all more rhythmic than either Leigh or I could attempt to copy. Once the service eventually ended, we realised they had prepared a lunch for us. I remembered Mookie, the dog in Romania who had fallen foul of undercooked meat at a BBQ. So, for me, caution was the order of the day. I do enjoy meat at home, but on missions and at BBQ, I am quite happy to 'go veggie'. I enjoyed all the salad and ate as much pineapple as I could. Leigh asked me if I had tried the Guinea fowl; I was quite happy to pass on that one. After the feast, we headed back to prepare for a busy Sunday of ministry.

The Sunday was a full programme in which Leigh and I were sent in different directions. I was honoured to go to the big church, headed up by Djakouti. Having been there 12 years previously with my brother, I knew what to expect. Times alone with the Lord at home prepare you for moments like this, when, as a single white person, in a congregation of hundreds of locals, you know the Lord is with you. That evening at our hotel, the girl at the reception said that she had been in the meeting and enjoyed my sermon. I was curious to see what she had gleaned from the service.

"Do you remember what I spoke about?" I asked her.

"Yes, vision and duty!" was her reply.

I felt a warm glow of God's favour as I heard her reply. Each church we visited was given guitars. I hoped that they would have the same longevity of use as the ones we had brought previously.

The following morning, Leigh didn't turn up at the time we agreed for breakfast. I went to his room to find him very sick, very weak and barely able to move. He had obviously got a very bad case of food poisoning. I phoned our hosts to tell them the situation and they came straight over. It's at times like this that I see the wisdom of travelling in pairs. I was glad I had responded to Leigh and joined him on this trip, because now his health and wellbeing were in my hands.

We managed to get Leigh into a private hospital, where he received the very best help available in that area. He had a very hard day fighting the infection. I was able to reassure him all that day that I was going nowhere and would be there for whatever he needed. Philomene came to the hospital to help with the communication and generally to ensure Leigh was the highest priority.

Leigh had to stay the night in hospital. The next day, 26 hours after being admitted, thankfully he was well enough to leave. Later that day, we flew home, very relieved that Leigh had made it through. After our visit, Philomene, our missionary, said, "You are the first white people to visit our church village, Akposso, in the plateau region of Togo. Imagine a choir and a community without a guitar? It is a missing link. Now we have your instrument, we are not only blessed but also we have sustainable tools to worship God and to impact the youth in the community."

Guitar Aid Hub

Remember that I was looking for premises for Guitar Aid? I enlisted the help of an architect who lived near me. He was so impressed with what the charity did that he agreed to give his services free of charge. The garage next to our house, which also belongs to us, would have the potential to house everything Guitar Aid needed to progress and prosper.

The plan was adventurous, stylish, large and detailed. It would need 30 tons of earth to be removed from the back of the garage, enabling the floor area to go back a further four metres. The plan included a second floor. What we were planning to build was more like a two-storey apartment. After a few visits from the planning department, we finally got the 'go ahead' for the work to start. The finished building definitely has the wow factor and is admired by all who visit it. It includes a store area, a showroom, an office and one of the best views over the city of Exeter.

For the official opening, we invited Marian's band, Timothy, to come to Exeter for a Guitar Aid celebration weekend. After a BBQ, Marian cut the tape and the new Guitar Aid Hub was open. I can't begin to tell you how much of a blessing it has been to have this facility right next door to my house. It hasn't cost Guitar Aid anything, as Liz and I funded it from part of the legacy of my mum and dad. A photo of them has pride of place there. Since its opening, hundreds of guitars have been given in memory of them. I am sure they would be pleased to think their legacy goes on. From the front view, it would be impossible to predict what lies behind. It's like entering the Tardis. Who would have believed the answer to Guitar Aid's next step would be right on my doorstep? No longer do I need to repair and restring guitars in my front room.

Generosity

The most significant feature of the new office is the inscription on the wall:

"You will be enriched so you can give even more generously. And when we take your gifts to those who need them, they will break out in thanksgiving to God." (2 Corinthians 9:11)

The theme of generosity has been in our DNA. The facility has greatly increased our giving. Many boxes of guitars have been sent out from there. It is a favourite place to go for my grandson Elias; he loves "next door". The Chesterfield sofa opposite the TV is his number one spot. While I work on guitars, he watches 'Toy Story' DVDs! I call him "the boss"! Elias likes to remove the brown paper that's wrapped around the strings of a new guitar; ripping it off one day, he turned to me and said, "Grandad, I love this job!"

My mum knew that having my own place for Guitar Aid was what I wanted. She heard my vision, she shared my plans and she saw it get started, but sadly she passed away before it was completed. The legacy of my mum and dad lives on in the vision of Guitar Aid. In my parents' generation, you would never refer to them by their first names, so the memory is to Pastor F.J.B. Sumner & Mrs H.J. Sumner. Those are the names written on the sound-hole label of hundreds of guitars. These instruments will be used to glorify God for many years to come and will ensure that Mum and Dad's names will be seen by future generations.

A Christian walk holds many ups and downs. Through it all, we are called to press on in the joy of our Lord. However, in our Father's kingdom we have people like Dave of Guitar Aid, who love to facilitate "Thy kingdom come" and surprise you with JOY. I am joyfully the recipient of a lovely guitar from him, for use in the Middle East, Dubai. Thank you, Dave, for the pleasant, joyful experience, and we can assure you it will be used to lift the name of our Lord Jesus Christ in this region.

Pastor Mathew Joseph
Dubai

Take the Next Step

23

Three unusual mission trips

Being 'the guitar man', I'm always thinking of how I can bless people with instruments, especially if a new country is involved. On holiday in Morocco, I took a guitar for a missionary there. Going on holiday with Liz to Portugal, I went one better. I have a good friend, Geoff Tresize, who lives there. Geoff has long been a supporter of Guitar Aid. I had sent guitars out to him, and he made contact with many of the churches there to see where they were needed. Now, I arranged with Liz that on the Sunday, from after breakfast until the evening of that day, we would be not only on holiday but also on mission! At first, Liz wasn't sure how this would work, but she was happy to go along with it.

Portugal

Geoff picked us up after breakfast. First stop was the International Church at Lagos. Wow! We shared our vision, gave a guitar and joined in the enthusiastic worship. On to the next one: Awana children's ministry, led by the charismatic Andre Mendes. We immediately felt the warmth of his friendship. Another guitar passed on. Then, we went to the AOG church for an afternoon service, where two guitars were given. Our final stop was with a group from house churches to round off the day.

All in all, it was an extremely busy day. We arrived back at our hotel just in time to have our evening meal, reflecting on a wonderful day meeting Christians, missionaries and young people from the churches in Portugal. Six more guitars given, six more opportunities to worship. I was glad we had made time in the middle of our holiday for this. I honour

Liz's willingness to support my desire to give wherever possible, even on holiday!

Riverside Kenya

I wrote earlier of Rose Lille, who encouraged me so much when I needed premises for Guitar Aid. Rose had an incredible vision, but not only that, she had the ability to get things done. One time when she went home to Kisumu, Kenya, she decided she would build a church in her home village. We heard from her how she had purchased a piece of land and intended to build what was going to be 'Riverside Kenya'. The level of faith she had for this project was outstanding. God honoured her faith, and she was given money from completely unexpected sources. Rose had been one of the stewards at Riverside and always made you feel welcome when you arrived. She completed the work of having Riverside Kenya built, and the church was opened. I would often say to Rose, "One day, I will be with you in Kenya and see your church." So, quite often I would say "one day" to Rose.

Riverside mission's team decided to plan a trip to Kenya to help in the church and build an outdoor kitchen that would feed the children of the village. I was very keen to put my name on the list of those going. When we turned up at the airport, they all laughed to see me with two large boxes full of guitars. Rose was already in Kenya when we left. The rest of the team met up with her when we arrived. The whole mission was a wonderful blend of the practical and the spiritual. Tim went out on the streets with an interpreter to do some evangelism. Bernie and Paul set about the task of getting the materials and equipment needed to build the kitchen. They spent each day sweating under the hot sun, building a functional kitchen.

While this was going on, Janet and I would be in the church helping with a conference for the church members and others who came along. There was a glass panel on the pulpit, and in the reflection I could see Bernie and Paul hard at work. The doors of the church were open, letting the sound out. While the two were working, they said they enjoyed listening to the worship songs. They particularly liked the fact that they knew all of them.

On the Sunday, it was my privilege to preach the word at the main service. As visitors, we were thrilled to hear them sing, dance and worship. For me, the most fulfilling thing was to be there with Rose and fulfil the promise that I had made to visit her church. She kept saying that she could hardly believe it had happened – a team from Riverside Exeter visiting Riverside Kenya! After the Sunday service, the kitchen was commissioned. What a sight to see two massive pots boiling and children eagerly awaiting the food that they needed so much! Mission accomplished!

The guitars were given, much to the delight of the recipients. They managed to find rhythms in Africa that we can't quite achieve back home. We loved the whole area of Kisumu and took advantage of the opportunity to have a boat trip on Lake Victoria. The plan was that we would return two years later, but we were unaware of world events that were soon to unfold.

Trying to get to Belarus

We left home at 5.45 am, the second week of March 2020, heading north on the M5 on a mission to Belarus. At about 6.20 we started to feel a vibration, which was getting worse as we neared Bristol. We pulled into Gordano services to realise we had a big problem. One of our tyres was completely flat. It would be impossible for us to continue on the motorway. We tried ringing anyone we could think of, but at 6.30 in the morning, no one was interested in helping.

We managed to limp slowly round to Avonmouth, the car now physically shaking! We rang many 24-hour services, eventually finding one around the corner. Looking at our tyre, we realised we were going nowhere! Someone eventually arrived at 8.10, but they said they didn't open until 8.30; £20 did the trick, though, and they started fitting a new tyre immediately. It occurred to us that had this happened anywhere else, we could have been in serious trouble. Leaving at 8.30, with our flight just three hours away, we hoped and prayed for favour. It seemed like everything was against us: roadworks, hold-ups, queues, you name it...

We arrived at the airport car park, after a difficult search, at 11.30. Arriving so close to the plane's departure time, both John and I were shaking. We boarded the transfer bus; totally dejected, realising we would miss our flight. We both had that sick, 'gutted' feeling and realised we would have to contact Dima in Belarus to tell him what had happened.

We told Dima that we weren't going to make it, but he was already halfway on a four-hour journey to pick us up and decided to wait to see if things changed.

Arriving at the airport, we loaded the guitars onto a trolley, to go for a flight we had missed. I turned to John and said, "Though the fig tree doesn't blossom, though there is no fruit on the vine, yet I will trust in the God of my salvation." I was quoting an abbreviation of Habakkuk 3:17-18.[7] This was a firm declaration of faith in God.

We contacted the travel agent and found it was not possible to change our flights. The Lufthansa desk confirmed that we were going nowhere, and we felt a sense of despair, as it seemed our mission was over. John was completely exhausted with the whole process and sat down. I continued to pace the floor, praying frantically for a breakthrough.

One more time, we returned to the Lufthansa desk. "Please, is there anything you can possibly do for us?" We were really desperate at this point.

"Just a minute..."

We waited.

"You can catch the next flight to Frankfurt. You have ten minutes to get checked in, and you will be in time for your connection flight to Belarus."

We could hardly believe our ears! Mad panic set in; we exchanged some cash for new tickets and 'legged it' to the check-in. We phoned Dima to tell him not to go home; we were coming after all... on the same flight we had originally agreed to be on!

Hindered but not defeated

Arriving in the connection lounge in Frankfurt in time for our connection was incredible. The relief, the joy, the excitement, the anticipation all hit us as we boarded that flight. Again, it was a case of 'hindered but not defeated'. When we finally arrived, Dima said it was really a miracle that we had made it.

---

[7] "Even though the fig trees have no blossoms, and there are no grapes on the vines; even though the olive crop fails, and the fields lie empty and barren; even though the flocks die in the fields, and the cattle barns are empty, yet I will rejoice in the Lord! I will be joyful in the God of my salvation!" (Habakkuk 3:17-18, NLT)

Going through customs with boxes of guitars was easy! They fully understood and appreciated what we were doing and seemed quite happy for us to go on unhindered. What an answer to prayer!

During our time in Belarus, we had many opportunities to speak and share in churches that were receiving guitars. Belarus had been in turmoil during this year due to the elections. Later, watching the demonstrations on TV, we were further reminded of how blessed we had been to go on this mission.

Arriving back at Heathrow, the airport was almost empty. During our time away, the world had changed.

Take the Next Step

Guitar Aid represents for us an initiative of praise to God, because of their attitude of love. Through Guitar Aid, every moment can be a special chord in our ministry in Portugal, where every month we can present new songs to the kids, and each year hoping to be a symphony to God. We are thankful to Guitar Aid for helping us be instruments tuned to God, in a tone of special worship where kids can know, love and serve God.

Pastor Andre Mendes
Awana, Portugal

Take the Next Step

24

A change of era

The last prophetic word my mum gave to me, the day she passed away, was, "God is going to lead you in a different way, but with the same results." This seemed very strange at the time, but it would eventually make sense. It was not just to be an era of change, but a change of era. Soon we would find ourselves unable to travel.

The pandemic

Early in 2020, just before our trip to Belarus, word was going around about a virus in China. Our government was playing it down as nothing too serious and nothing that was going to affect us. John and I had planned to go to Belarus, and there seemed to be no reason to change our plans.

When we returned from the mission, we were immediately hit by lockdown. "Stay at home" was the message, with churches, restaurants and shops all being closed. We were so thankful we hadn't missed the trip to Belarus, and also that Guitar Aid has its base at my home. With travel restrictions in place, I realised that I wouldn't be going anywhere. My prayer was, "What can I do next?"

We started to get requests for guitars on a weekly basis during lockdown. We responded to each request, resulting in hundreds of guitars being sent out during this time of no travel. We couldn't go, but our guitars could be sent. Austria, Slovakia, Poland, Hungary, Romania, Serbia, Bulgaria, Italy, Czech Republic, Albania, Kenya, Uganda and even as far as India, were just some of the nations we sent guitars to. This was a time of sowing into the kingdom of God. This was just what my mum had prophesied: a different way of operating, but with the same results.

The two Terrys

Terry Mills was a lad from Exeter that we tried to encourage. In his early teens, he sang in the worship band at Riverside Church. Terry was very enthusiastic in all he did. In the evenings, he ran a disco, and he was a favourite at the school our children went to. His involvement in entertainment led to him having a top agency for celebrities. Big Talent Group had many very famous people on their books.

Before this took off, when Terry was still in his teens, John decided it would be good to invite Terry to come along with us to Romania. I remember that when we were driving through Frankfurt, we saw a plane about to land. Terry asked, "What is that?" and we replied that it was a plane about to land. His response was classic: "It's too low to land!" That was our Terry!

When the pandemic came and it was no longer possible to travel, Terry got to hear about how many guitars we were shipping at this difficult time. I received a call from his PR manager, who said that Terry wanted to run a story on what Guitar Aid was doing. They even managed to contact Sir Cliff Richard, who commented that it was amazing how we were able to get this large quantity of guitars to those who needed them. At this time, Terry decided to go on a business trip to Mexico and sadly passed away due to contracting Covid. It was such a shock to us all. But Terry always lived for the moment and would never miss any opportunity to promote Big Talent Group. We had heard the statistics of 160,000 people dying of Covid, but now it hit home to us that each would be a person like Terry – loved and who would be greatly missed.

At a similar time, our friend Terry Harris, who had travelled many thousands of miles with us in the Land Rover, also went into hospital and contracted Covid, which led to him too passing away. Such were the restrictions at that time that John and I were unable to visit him while he was in hospital. We were, however, able to give Terry a big surprise in the last year of his life before this happened. We arranged for Pastor Janos from Hungary to come over for a surprise visit to see him. Terry's reaction when Janos knocked on his door was priceless! We all went and enjoyed breakfast together. For Terry to be back with me, John and Janos was the thing that gave him the greatest pleasure.

I vividly remember one time when Terry Harris gave his testimony in Poland. He told how overnight, as he committed his life to Jesus, his desire to smoke had immediately left. Terry had been a heavy smoker. The response to this was incredible. Without being asked, people from the congregation came forward and threw down their packets of cigarettes. Their desire to have the same deliverance as Terry was clearly evident. I don't think I've ever witnessed anything like this where the desire to 'lay something down on the altar' was demonstrated in such a widespread and public way.

Wrong Passport!

We travelled together, many thousands of miles, John, Terry and me. They called us the three musketeers! We always watched each other's backs as a matter of course.

On one occasion, we arrived at the border between Hungary and Romania and handed our passports in to be checked… John Sumner, David Sumner, Cilla Harris… *Cilla?* Who is Cilla? Terry had managed to travel all the way to Romania from the UK via France, Belgium, Germany, Austria and Hungary, without any problem, on his wife's passport!

"It can't be Cilla's passport; my passport is always on top and I took the top one…"

But Terry had forgotten to check inside. He was not going into Romania without his own passport.

"They are being mean to me. Don't they realise I haven't been well?"

But there was no way Terry was going any further. What could he do? John and I both said simultaneously, "DHL" We had seen an advert saying DHL could ship anything anywhere in 24 hours. We called our friend Pastor Janos from Hungary to come and pick Terry up. Then we contacted Cilla and told her to take Terry's passport to DHL as soon as possible. It was Friday, so she had to wait until Monday to send it off.

Sure enough, the passport arrived on Tuesday, and Terry was able to finish the journey to Romania. From that time onwards, we always checked with each other that we had the right passport.

Serving by sending

For more than 30 years we have been building relationships and making friends in over 50 countries. It was those connections that enabled us to thrive during the pandemic. We were able to respond to all the requests for instruments, safe in the knowledge that we knew where they were going. We knew who they were going to and that they would be very much appreciated. On a regular basis, I packed up boxes of guitars and filled out the customs documents that are now needed since Brexit. There is also duty to be paid, as we are no longer part of the European Union. The additional cost has not stopped us. "What God orders, he pays for."

The years of 2020/21 proved to be difficult for many people across the globe. Having an event-driven lifestyle, I would always know when my next mission was, and probably the next few. 2020 was intended to be a year of celebrating 30 years of Guitar Aid. Trips had been planned to Uganda, Hungary, Slovakia, Kenya. It was going to be a year of many missions – and then the pandemic struck.

One day, I was walking by the River Exe, halfway through the pandemic restrictions, and I asked God, "Where am I going?"

The reply was clear: "Nowhere."

Instead, I felt God lead me to Psalm 37:7: "Be still in the presence of the Lord, and wait patiently for him to act." Being still and waiting patiently was not something I was used to. During the months that followed, however, I began to realise the benefits of being still in God's presence and waiting patiently for him to act.

For someone who loves going here, there and everywhere, the waiting and being still was out of my comfort zone, but nonetheless very much the way God was leading. These times of waiting and praying produced the fruit of patience. During lockdown, I got around to fixing guitars that had been waiting for the right moment for my attention. Being stuck at home wasn't so bad after all.

Although we could have no direct contact with our friends on missions, here is one story of someone in our church we were able to help during lockdown, Joseph Harris:

"Guitar Aid has always been something close to my heart since I came to Exeter. When I met Dave and got to hear stories of him sending guitars all across the globe, I was amazed. During my year interning at the church, I sent Dave a message asking if I could

borrow a guitar. In typical Dave Sumner fashion, he went above and beyond and drove round to where I was living, and gifted me a guitar. At the height of lockdown and Covid, I had never picked up a guitar; however, thanks to the generosity of Guitar Aid and Dave, I started to learn how to play the guitar by watching YouTube videos and ended up spending hours trapped inside. This guitar not only provided me with an outlet to cope with the anxiety of life during Covid-19, but also allowed me to worship God. As a drummer, I found it hard to worship during Covid, and this guitar was an amazing way of me being able to worship God from my bedroom. Since then, I have gone on to play at church. I wouldn't be where I am spiritually if it were not for the generosity I experienced through the work Guitar Aid does."

Remembering God's promises

During the times of Covid-19, we learned to communicate on Zoom. Church was online instead of in person, and we all had to adapt to the restrictions being imposed on us, nationally and internationally.

Waiting patiently and being still in God's presence has its advantages. You start to reflect on prophetic words God has given you. Mum's words, that God would lead me in a different way but with the same results, started to make sense. In those quiet times, I would often visit Exeter Cathedral and spend time praying and quietly reflecting. For it was at Exeter Cathedral that I had received one of the most powerful prophetic words I have ever had. Holy Trinity Brompton (HTB) were holding a special service there. It was a time when God was pouring out his Spirit in a special way at HTB. Rev. Sandy Miller was speaking; he spoke with such dignity, such authority and incredible anointing. He said that his team would be praying for people that night. When he finished, he came down from the pulpit and walked towards me. He held out his hands and started to prophesy over me. I felt a rush of the Holy Spirit come over me, and I would never forget his words: "God is going to lead you to many countries, places far from here. There is no place that will be closed to you; you will travel to distant lands for the kingdom." It was amazing to hear these words. Can you see why I go back to that spot to pray?

Another great memory I have of Exeter Cathedral is of when I was invited to have a Guitar Aid display at an event called 'Unity in Diversity'.

This event was headed up by Matt Redman. I love the worship songs Matt has written. It further confirmed to me the power of the guitar in worship when Matt sang 'Facedown' with his guitar to a totally packed-out cathedral. He was going on a mission the very next week, so I invited him to take whatever guitars he wanted from the display to go with him. He picked four guitars from the ones I had there. Matt has been an advocate of Guitar Aid since the early 90s.

A family crisis

Not only did the pandemic stop us in our tracks and prevent us from going on missions, a family crisis was to hit us that would ensure that we would be going nowhere for a while.

As a family, we met for Christmas in 2021, sharing that wonderful time of the year together, unaware that we were about to face the most difficult time of our entire lives. Just before Christmas, I had been asked to preach at church and spoke on 'Facing Life's Challenges'. I used the scripture Habakkuk 3:17-19, which you may remember from the story of when John and I missed our plane. When sharing this message, I had no idea that Liz and I would need to trust God deeply in the circumstances that lay ahead.

On Wednesday 29th December, Chris' wife Kate rang us to say Chris was really poorly. We immediately went over and said, "You must ring 999." We stayed with them until the ambulance took Chris to hospital.

On Thursday 30th December, they called to say that Chris was critical and we needed a miracle. They thought he would not make it through the night. We were desperate, and we got on our knees, crying before God, tears rolling down our faces, praying like never before for our son.

In the utter desperation that we were feeling, I sensed a breakthrough and clearly felt God saying to me, "He's going to make it, he's going to make it." I turned to Liz and told her that we must hold on to these words and trust God whatever the circumstances. I then sent a message to Pastor Aran and he sent us a scripture that was to be a rock to us during the coming days and months:

"This I declare about the Lord; he alone is my refuge, my place of safety; he is my God and I will trust him. For he will rescue you from every trap and protect you from deadly disease. Do not be afraid of the terrors of the night, nor the arrow that flies in the day. Do not dread the disease that stalks the darkness, nor the disaster that strikes at midday. Though a thousand fall at your side, though ten thousand are dying around you, these evils will not touch you."[8]

These verses became a source of comfort; we read the whole psalm every day. At this stage of the pandemic, over 160,000 people had died from Covid in the UK. We just kept holding on to the promise, "He's going to make it."

As we were praying, I was reminded of the nobleman who came to Jesus, and Jesus said, "What would you have me do?" The reply was, "That my son may be healed." We similarly wanted Jesus to ask us that question, to which our reply would also be, "That our son may be healed."

Liz and I spent many nights praying. She would pray until about 5 am, and then I would take over. We stood in agreement for a miracle, often having communion together, reminding God of the covenant relationship we have with him.

On the 10th of January, we were called to say goodbye to Chris. Pastor Aran was with us as the doctors gave us news of little hope. We had to put on the full Covid protection gear, the same as the hospital staff were wearing – but as we entered the room where he was, our faith began to rise.

At this moment, he was barely alive. I touched his forehead and prayed, "Same power, same Spirit, same anointing," and as I did, I felt electricity flow through my body. We spoke life and healing into that situation. We left the room believing for a miracle and full of faith.

Aran said something that really helped us: "Imagine the chairs around your table; one of them is for faith to sit in. Faith and fear cannot sit together, so when fear comes, it will leave if faith takes its place. The chair is for one or the other." Many times we thought of this, and when any fear came, we commanded it to go, sitting on the chair, declaring our home a 'house of faith'.

The valley of the shadow of death

Psalm 23 speaks about the "valley of the shadow of death". Liz and I have been in that valley on several occasions. They told us that if Chris

---

[8] Psalm 91:2-7

had not been so young (34 years of age), they would have turned the machines off.

One time while praying, God gave Liz a vision of Chris and Kate together. Many times, they told us that only a miracle could save him. We responded with our faith and said that we believed in miracles. One consultant, bringing us more bad news, said, "If you believe in the God of the universe and he is going to help you, then I will do everything I possibly can to help." This was music to our ears. We had to face the painful wait of a brain scan, a heart scan and various different tests, each time holding on to the promise, "He is going to make it."

After nine weeks of Chris being in the Intensive Care Unit on a ventilator, we started to witness a miracle. He had his tracheotomy removed, had his feeding tube removed and he was put on a normal ward. The journey of recovery had started. First Chris had kidney failure, then his kidneys were working again; he battled through pneumonia, sepsis, Covid and organ failure. One significant moment in the recovery process was when Chris was wheeled out to see us on a visit; he couldn't speak because he had a tracheostomy, but mouthed the words, "I love you" to me and Liz. This was such a joy to witness. That evening I watched the sunset at Exeter Quay with tears in my eyes. The words of the old hymn came flooding into my thoughts.

> *Heaven above is softer blue,*
> *Earth around is sweeter green;*
> *Something lives in every hue*
> *Christless eyes have never seen:*
> *Birds with gladder song overflow,*
> *Flowers with deeper beauty shine,*
> *Since I know, as now I know,*
> *I am his and he is mine.*

That evening, everything in the world seemed more vivid, more beautiful to me.

Eventually, at Easter, Chris was admitted to a specialist rehabilitation centre in Exeter, called the 'Mardon' unit. The treatment there was exactly what was needed. Each week, Chris had a programme of tasks to help achieve the ultimate goal of going home.

We could see the light at the end of the tunnel when we visited Chris in mid-July. He actually made us a cup of tea. It was the best 'cuppa' ever! We knew he was getting closer to coming home when a few days later he turned up at our house in the car with Kate. This was the first time he had seen our home since Christmas six-and-a-half months before. The Mardon centre, where Chris was having rehabilitation, were so pleased with his progress that they let him try to get into the car. He said that it was no problem and that they had driven down to Exmouth to see the sea. Chris didn't get out of the car there, but nonetheless this was progress.

After seven-and-a-half months in hospital and rehabilitation, he finally came home for good. That's 227 days – a very long time! We rejoiced in the miracle that had taken place. After having had so many praying to this end, finally the day had arrived – Chris home, just in time for his 35th birthday. Praise God for his faithfulness!

During the time of praying and believing for Chris' miracle, there is one album that was an incredible blessing to both Liz and me: *Stained Glass Stories* by Philippa Hanna. The songs on that album ministered to us at a time when we needed it most. The song 'You're Still God' was a favourite of ours; we listened to it many times with tears in our eyes. The way this album helped was even more special, knowing that Philippa endorses Guitar Aid.

It's beautiful to see how God cares. I am very happy that I know Dave from Guitar Aid, and I was honoured to spend time with him at Campfest. Guitar Aid doesn't serve only worship leaders by supporting them with guitars, but it is mainly a service that blows fire of worship all across the globe. Guitar Aid has been standing by me and the ministry of my band ESPE for years, and I'm so thankful for it.

Julo Slovak
ESPE band, Godzone project
Slovakia

25

The work continues

Through the many years we have been giving instruments, the quality of the guitars we give has definitely improved, but the basic vision of what Guitar Aid stands for hasn't changed. In 1990, the vision was to supply instruments of worship to those who needed them so that the name of Jesus could be lifted up across the globe. Our original Missions Statement still stands true today:

"Worldwide vision to release and empower others to worship, by providing instruments to those unable to obtain or afford them."

We are investing in the lives of the individuals that receive our instruments. We have good friends, Keith and Val Tipple, who have spent their lives involved in ministry both here and in the USA. When they came to see the Guitar Aid hub, Val made a lovely comment. She said, "You are worship enablers."

I really like that thought..

Seeing a vision take shape

While going through the difficult time trusting God for Chris' recovery, I clearly felt God was telling me that the next step for me on missions would not be shown until I had got through the situation with Chris. Once Chris was out of the main hospital and into the rehabilitation centre, I felt a sense of relief and started to talk to John about planning a trip to Hungary and Romania. John also had to consider the timing of this carefully, having been in hospital himself for five weeks after having a major operation. With Chris steadily improving and John now able to do so much more, the time had come to respond again to the call to

"Go!" During the pandemic, we had sometimes wondered when this time would come...

Returning again to Hungary had always been high on our list of priorities. The thought of sitting at a café with Pastor Janos – drinking coffee, eating cake – had helped us through the difficult times of the pandemic, when travel seemed a distant memory and the thought of meeting up was an impossibility. Here we were again, thanking God that once again we were taking up his call on our lives to go on missions.

We have a long-term relationship with the Roma community in Hungary. The last time we had been here, Pastor Janos had taken us to see Laszlo, who is the president of the Hungarian Roma Mission. Laszlo invited us to preach and sing at Mezbereni, one of the village churches. Church was held in a house where two rooms had been knocked into one to accommodate the meeting. The place was absolutely packed out. The atmosphere was electric, as young and old alike danced, laughed and sang at the tops of their voices. Laszlo told of his vision to have a purpose-built church in the village. On our most recent trip, we had taken more guitars along to the Roma Mission Headquarters in Bekes.

Now Pastor Laszlo said that he would like to show us something. He drove us to that same village, where the vision had now become a reality. Right in the centre of the street where the meeting was held stood a brand-new church, well underway to becoming the first Roma Temple in the Pentecostal churches of Hungary.

Laszlo told us the story of how he had obtained the land. It was owned by one of the local mafia. Laszlo went to meet him and told him God had given him a vision to build a church on the land. The mafia man immediately agreed to give him the land for nothing. He only then found out that his wife had sold the land behind his back to the local council. So Laszlo then approached the council, who agreed to sell the land to him at a fraction of its value in order that a church could be built.

We felt truly blessed to be witnessing the fulfilment of a vision. I am so glad that for many years we have been able to support the vison of the Roma Mission, and Laszlo in particular.

Serving by staying behind

Especially in the early years of missions, it would have been impossible to do what we have done without the support of our wives. They stayed at home, looking after our children while we followed the call of God on our lives. This was before mobile phones, and communication was difficult; sometimes it took days before we could let our families know where we were or how we were doing. For me, the support Liz has given has been so valuable.

It has not always been easy. Many times things would go wrong while I was away, like the time water started pouring into the living room from the burst pipe upstairs, or when the key broke in the lock as Liz came home from church, now unable to get in until Bill Hill helped her. You might also recall the story about Daniel breaking his leg just before we went on a mission.

Talking about Daniel, he caused a scene one time. We were gathered together outside our home, ready to go on mission. We said our goodbyes and left. Then he started shouting. "You naughty mummy, you made my daddy go away. You let my daddy come home!" (He was probably about five at this time.) He kept repeating this, louder and louder. It doesn't take much to imagine what the neighbours must have been thinking!

Dave Griffiths said, "25 years... Don't tell me there haven't been sacrifices along the way," and he was right. Yes, there *have* been sacrifices, and most of them have been made by our wives. It's only now that I fully realise how difficult it must have been looking after four young children while your husband is in foreign parts perusing the call of God on his life. I honour the support Liz has given me through the years.

To the ends of the earth

The furthest we have ever sent a guitar is Kona, Hawaii. We had a girl in our church, Georgia, who was on a Youth With A Mission discipleship training course in Hawaii. Having given up a year to serve on the mission, when she sent me a request, I wanted to encourage her and respond in a positive way. Her best friend on the mission team, Naomi Fierro, needed to replace her broken guitar. Here is her story:

> *"The headstock of my guitar broke and I was super heartbroken. I didn't know what to do. I'm here at YWAM Kona, I'm part of the music track and that involves playing my guitar. The guitar that broke was the one that I have had since I was 11. I didn't know what to do, so I decided to go before Jesus, telling him, 'I believe this is what you want me to do, and this is what you called me for. So I'm trusting you are going to provide for my needs and*

accomplish what you have set before me.' Being a student at YWAM, I don't have money to buy a guitar, so I gave it to Jesus. Within 24 hours he answered and today this guitar arrived! I want to say a huge thank you to Guitar Aid and Dave Sumner. I'm blessed beyond measure for the support that has been given me, to go to the nations and show the love of Jesus through music and song-writing. I'm so pleased, so happy and super excited!"

A confirmation

One of the guitars we give has a scripture on the headstock. I considered that with different models of consumer items, they often have an inscription – Mark 1, Mark 2 and so on. My favourite amplifier of all time is a Mesa Boogie Mark 2. With the guitar I thought, "Let's go straight to Mark 16, and in particular Mark 16 verse 15!"

And he told them, "Go into all the world and preach the good news to everyone."

After giving one of these guitars, the pastor receiving it noticed the scripture. With excitement he rang us. "Would you believe it? The scripture on the guitar is the very passage I spoke on this morning! This is a wonderful confirmation to me that I am doing what God wants." It was an encouragement to us too.

30 years of the Haven of Hope orphanage

What a privilege it was to be invited to the opening of the Haven of Hope over 30 years ago! What an even greater privilege it was to be invited to the 30th anniversary celebrations! This was an event not to be missed.

The invite came from Pastor Moise Pop and his wife Nuti. They have faithfully taken charge of the orphanage and the church for many years. Pastor Moise is a wonderful example of working and serving. He has held a full-time job with the local electric company in order to sustain and support both the church and the orphanage.

There were four of us from Exeter that were invited to this celebration: Gemma, who spent 11 years living at the orphanage; John and I, who have both been involved since 1991; and Matt Jackson, who first went to the orphanage with John in 2014 and has been two or three times a year since then. During the celebration, Matt managed to do his sermon completely in Romanian, something John and I have never achieved.

For me, the highlight was seeing young adults that now had families and homes of their own, who had started their journey years ago in that very orphanage. "They were just little children when we first met them; look at them now!" We spent time in the homes of two brothers who we remembered as little boys. I look at the next generation coming into the home, and I have the same hope for them to go on and achieve the best they can for God.

The success is down to the faithfulness and perseverance of Pastor Moise and his wife Nuti. At the moment, the orphanage has 19 children they are looking after. We love the original name given to the orphanage, the 'Haven of Hope'; it truly has given hope to many who have come from a hopeless situation.

Albanian generosity

Just before Covid, our plan had been to return to Albania. As soon as travel restrictions eased, it was firmly back on our 'must do' list. We had stayed in touch with Ralf Gjoni throughout the years, and he agreed to plan our itinerary. Ralf is a well-respected public figure in Albania, having served as an MP for many years. For the past decade, he had fought against corruption and injustice, bringing a Christian perspective to politics.

We took 14 guitars, three ukuleles and lots of drum sticks. We visited churches, youth groups and worship teams, passing on the much-needed instruments. During our time in Tirana, we were interviewed for Christian radio about our visit. We spent a day with Rachel Wilson, the AOG missionary, and saw the excellent children's work she is involved in up in the north of Albania.

The main purpose of our visit was to go back to Pogradec, where we had first gone in 1992. We met up with Arnold, the German missionary who had now been our friend for three decades. During this time, he told us that over 40 million pounds' worth of aid had come to Albania, channelled through Nehemiah charity. It was a delight to meet up with Andi, who had been baptised as a 17-year-old youth back in 1992 and was still following Jesus now at the age of 47.

On the Sunday, we went to the church that had been planted as a result of that first mission with AOG GB and the German team. As I spoke in the church about our vision, I looked into the congregation and spotted Arnold. Seeing him there reminded me of his years of faithfulness.

Wherever we gave guitars, they were received with gratitude and an overwhelming sense of appreciation. The church also captured my vision, so much so that the pastor asked them to take up an offering for Guitar Aid. Would you believe it? A church in Albania, one of the poorest countries in Europe, collected 250 euros. I could hardly believe it! It goes to show that generosity is not dependent on your circumstances or your resources; it is an attitude of heart. I saw a spirit of generosity in this church that reminded me that God is our provider and he will bless us from unexpected sources.

30-year 'catch up' in Romania

On a recent trip to Romania, I wanted to visit the exact place where I had caught the vision for missions and Guitar Aid ministry had started.

I stood on that spot thinking, "33 years ago we arrived with three lorry-loads of aid..." I thanked God for the way that trip had changed my life, and the 4,000 plus people that had been impacted by receiving instruments from Guitar Aid.

"Take a photo of me standing here," I said to my brother John.

He also wanted a photo, as this was the place he had first visited in January 1990.

Just then, in perfect English, a voice said, "Would you like me to take a picture of you both?"

As we stood together to have our photo taken, I noticed the car behind the person had a registration 'ARDIU'.

"You're an Ardiu, aren't you?"

"Yes, I'm Elvis."

We hadn't seen Elvis for over 30 years, and in fact it was Elvis' home that we had stayed in on that first visit in 1990. Elvis had been a six-year-old boy then! We told him that we were visiting his uncle, and could he come back in an hour?

"For sure!" was the reply.

I often meet up with friends for a coffee and a catch-up, but this was no ordinary catch-up; there were 30 years of catching up to do!

Elvis told us that he had been following our missions on Facebook. "I've watched you going to Egypt, Cuba, Cambodia and Kenya..." but now we were having face-to-face fellowship. These chance meetings are often 'God moments' that will stay in our memories for years to come.

Finally getting to Rwanda

Something happened on our first mission to Kenya that left a lasting impression on me. It was not long after the genocide in Rwanda. The Bible College in Nairobi, that would usually be full of Kenyan students, had been overwhelmed with refugees escaping the horrors that had become the norm in Rwanda. Hearing firsthand from people that had narrowly escaped left us disturbed in our spirits and wondering how such massive loss of life could happen. Although that was many years ago, the impression it had made hadn't faded.

Our pastor's wife, Rachel, came to a missions meeting, telling how God had laid a country on her heart: *Rwanda!* Something in my spirit leapt. As soon as she said it, not only did I know she would follow the vision through, but that I would be going on that mission. So the mission happened, with twelve members of Riverside Exeter.

The best way to understand a country is to know some of its history. A visit to the Kigali Genocide Museum dramatically shows the horrific past that the country has emerged from. Clearly, lessons have been learned, as now a spirit of peace, harmony and understanding can be clearly seen. The children in the project we visited were happy, contented and cared for. What a transformation has taken place in this country!

After many visits to Africa, it was here that I had my first experience of a proper safari in an open top four-by-four. As a worshipper of God, it's truly enriching to see the wonders of his creation and so many animals in their natural environment.

The climax of the mission was a crusade, with over 3,000, where we worshipped using Guitar Aid instruments that would be later left in Rwanda. In most poor countries, children will ask for sweets, toys or money; in the poorer areas of Rwanda, they just simply ask for water. This shows the extent of the need there. For sure we will be back!

Kenya

In missions, as in many areas of life, keeping your word is a fundamental part of your integrity. I promised Mama Rose that the next time I went to Kenya, I would take my wife Liz with me. Unfortunately, Mama Rose passed away, but the promise remained. Not only did Liz go on the next mission to Kenya, but we were also able to take a commemorative plaque to dedicate Riverside Kenya to the memory of Mama Rose. Once again, the team were able to give contributions that were practical, spiritual and cultural.

One of the team members, James Kirby, a professional musician, illustrated the power one guitar has to engage a large audience, when he performed to a school of over 3,000 students, leaving them captivated and inspired by his unique style of playing. James sat next to me in one meeting; I had been sharing along with Pastor Aran, and the presence of God in that service was tangible. I looked out of the church window, and in the distance I could see some of our team doing practical work. I also saw my wife Liz and others doing activities with the children. This was such a complete and diverse mission, enabling everyone to give from their own individual skills and abilities.

Just then, I noticed James writing on his phone. He had been inspired by Aran's talk to write a song. I will never forget the moment James sang that song. I acted as a microphone stand, holding the mic as still as possible, while he sang with such an anointing, with something that was birthed on his first mission.

Your name is higher than the mountains,
Your love is wider than the sea,
Your word is louder than thunder,
Your name empowers me.

Every time we sing that song, it reminds me of the impact it can have on your life, 'going on your first mission'.

John Sebunya, the Ugandan boy raised by monkeys

Since I first saw the programme about John, the boy brought up by monkeys in Uganda, I wanted to go and meet him to give him a new guitar. The way I saw him on TV using a blue Guitar Aid instrument, just by chance, reminds me that God is interested in the details of our lives.

Andy and Rachel David regularly go to Uganda with their charity World of Worth, and they worked hard to track John down. Although a planned trip to Uganda in 2020 had to be postponed, we agreed to go on a later trip to take John a new guitar.

A team of eight of us went, headed up by Andy, and including my son Ben. What a joy to share an African mission with one of my sons! One of the highlights was Ben and me leading worship together, both playing Guitar Aid instruments. We took ten guitars on this mission, but one of them was very special: a brand-new blue guitar for John.

We organised everything through Paul Wasswa, John's pastor, who also is involved in 'The Pearl of Africa' children's choir. It dawned on me that many years ago the choir had come to Exeter and I had given them a guitar; was this the one John ended up getting?

With much joy we met John and his pastor Paul. As I gave him his new guitar, words can't describe the sheer delight on his face. I hugged him and he snuggled into me as if I were his long-lost dad! It made me think, "This is one guitar, one story, but each of the 4,000 instruments we've given has its own story to tell." Is it any wonder I am so passionate about the ministry of Guitar Aid?

The journey continues

I count it an honour to be a missionary with AOG GB. In recent years, someone who has been a great source of encouragement and inspiration is Pastor Kirk McAtear, who is now the AOG GB Missions Director. Kirk is a true missionary, having left Australia with his family with the call of God on his life for the UK and Europe. The prayer support that Liz and I received during the most difficult times with our son Chris was outstanding.

The AOG national leadership team and the missions team prayed regularly for us. We thank God for the miracle that has taken place. The member care group headed up by Hanna Prosser has also been a great blessing at a time when we needed encouragement and support.

During the pandemic, Steve Prosser invited me to join the AOG Europe Missions team. Regularly, I meet on Zoom with Steve and Sasha Vitakic from Serbia, and together we plan how best to support and encourage our missionaries in Europe. Being part of the AOG Missions family is a great blessing, and I am sure I will have many more years working for God's kingdom with these amazing people. Someone who came to our church several years ago, Pastor Arthur Ireson, said something that has always inspired my faith: "How God has led you in the past is a good indication of how he is going to lead you in the future."

Lord, lead me on!

"It's not for you to know the end, or yet to see the path, but to see the next step and take it."

These, my mum's words, were quoted at the start of this book. I pray that from what you have read here, you will be inspired to look at what *you* have in your hands, commit it to God and find the next step that God has for you.

I would like to thank Brother David for bringing guitars to Ethiopia, and thanks to those who support Guitar Aid, we are very glad. Since we have had guitars in the church, our worship has not been the same; it has changed. Young people are coming because of this. Having the guitar has enabled us to start two choirs. Thank you on behalf of the church; thank you so much; may God richly bless you.

Bishop Teklu Wolde
Ethiopia

Take the Next Step

Appendix 1: Memorable quotes

There are several sayings I have that most people who know me will have heard me quote at times. Here are a few:

> Going to church is like having a roast chicken meal. You have to eat the meat and leave the bones.

Many make the mistake of chewing on bones. There is plenty of meat in the church to give you all the spiritual nourishment you need. Don't focus on things that you are meant to leave on the side.

> Missions are usually inconvenient, but rarely impossible.

So often we can find reasons why not to go on a mission or follow what God is calling us to do. Once we realise that whatever we do will be inconvenient to someone, we can process that, find what is needed to overcome it and proceed with God's blessing.

> On your first mission, at worst you could have a bad holiday; at best you could find the call of God on your life for missions.

I like to encourage people that the first mission they go on is the most important, as they will find out if God is leading them into this area for the future.

> If a guitar is not good enough for me to play, then I won't give it.

To me, it's important for the right guitars to go to the right people. A guitar that is quite adequate for a home group may not be good enough for a worship leader in a large congregation. We want the guitars we give to reflect our aim of 'giving with generosity'.

> Be a fruit inspector.

On missions, you can often be put in a situation where you face something unfamiliar – maybe an individual, maybe a church. You might find yourself in a different denomination, a different culture and surrounded by a different language. In this situation, your best option is to inspect the fruit. It is good to assess how much good is coming from the situation before you.

> You never know how far your influence will go.

I have seen pictures appear on social media of Guitar Aid instruments being used in the most obscure and distant places, proving this saying to be true.

> Generosity is not dependent on your circumstances or resources; it is an attitude of the heart.

God wants us to be generous with what we have, whether it is little or much. In turn, he will bless us with more so we can be even more generous.

> The word of God is preached with passion by anointed pastors and leaders, irrespective of how poor the country is. Anointed and passionate musicians and worship leaders in the same situation are held back by the poor instruments and, in some cases, no instruments at all.

This is especially true in Africa; we have seen it in many places. Our vision is to change this situation so that worship and the word together make a difference.

> It's an opportunity for grace.

When someone does something unpleasant, or circumstances are not to your liking, accepting the situation will make you a more gracious person.

> You can have faith in a moment; faithfulness takes a little longer.

Having faith and being faithful sound similar, but they differ in how long it takes to accomplish them. True faithfulness can take a lifetime.

From early childhood, I dreamed of playing the electric guitar. Four years ago, when I was eleven, I came to this church. They had a worship team, with instruments supplied by Guitar Aid. I realised my dream could be realised at an early age, and so, my journey began.

Every day after school, I went to the church to practise. I learned things that at first seemed impossible. I remained true to my dream and kept going. I said to myself, "I believe through this God will do great things." Since then, I have had a great bold-ness and a desire to develop for the glory of God.

I believe this is only the beginning.

Julia Harhulyova
Gomel, Belarus

Take the Next Step

Appendix 2: Mission trips

Year	Month	Mission	Destination	Visit
1990	March	1	Romania	1
	October	2	Romania	2
1991	April	3	Romania	3
	October	4	Romania	4
	December	5	Romania	5
1992	July	6	Albania	1
	October	7	Romania	6
1993	March	8	Albania	2
	September	9	Albania	3
1994	July	10	Albania	4
	October	11	Armenia	1
1995	March	12	Romania	7
			Hungary	1
	October	13	Romania	8
			Hungary	2
			Czech Republic	1
			Poland	1
1996	March	14	Albania	5
	October	15	Romania	9
			Hungary	3
			Czech Republic	2
			Poland	2
1997	March	16	Jamaica	1
			Cuba	1
	July	17	Poland	3
	October	18	Bosnia	1
			Croatia	1
			Romania	10
			Hungary	4

Year	Month	Mission	Destination	Visit
1998	February	19	Poland	4
	May	20	Bosnia	2
			Croatia	2
	November	21	Romania	11
			Hungary	5
			Czech Republic	3
			Poland	5
1999	February	22	Croatia	3
	June	23	Albania	6
	October	24	Romania	12
			Hungary	6
			Czech Republic	4
2000	February	25	Turkey	1
	June	26	Kenya	1
			Tanzania	1
	November	27	Romania	13
			Hungary	7
2001	March	28	Romania	14
			Hungary	8
			Czech Republic	5
			Slovakia	1
			Poland	6
	May	29	Czech Republic	6
	June	30	Kenya	2
			Tanzania	2
	October	31	Romania	15
			Hungary	9
			Czech Republic	7
			Slovakia	2
			Poland	7
2002	March	32	Romania	16
			Hungary	10
			Croatia	4
	May	33	Ghana	1
	October	34	Romania	17
			Hungary	11
			Czech Republic	8
			Slovakia	3
			Poland	8

Year	Month	Mission	Destination	Visit
2003	February	35	Cambodia	1
		36	Romania	18
			Hungary	12
	July	37	Macedonia	1
			Kosovo	1
	October	38	Romania	19
			Hungary	13
			Croatia	5
2004	March	39	Romania	20
			Hungary	14
	May	40	USA	1
	July	41	Tanzania	3
	October	42	Romania	21
2005	January	43	Hungary	15
	March	44	Ukraine	1
	June	45	Cambodia	2
	October	46	Romania	22
			Hungary	16
			Czech Republic	9
			Slovakia	4
			Poland	9
2006	February	47	Ukraine	2
			Belarus	1
	May	48	Romania	23
			Hungary	17
			Czech Republic	10
			Slovakia	5
			Poland	10
	June	49	Burkina Faso	1
	October	50	Romania	24
			Hungary	18
			Czech Republic	11
			Slovakia	6
			Poland	11

Year	Month	Mission	Destination	Visit
2007	January	51	Hungary	19
	May	52	Romania	25
			Hungary	20
	June	53	Togo	1
			Ghana	2
	October	54	Romania	26
			Hungary	21
			Slovakia	7
			Poland	12
2008	February	55	Hungary	22
	May	56	Romania	27
			Hungary	23
	June	57	India	1
	October	58	Romania	28
			Hungary	24
			Moldova	1
2009	February	59	Hungary	25
		60	Romania	29
			Hungary	26
	June	61	Vietnam	1
			Philippines	1
	October	62	Romania	30
			Hungary	27
			Slovakia	8
			Poland	13
			Herzegovina	1
2010	March	63	Ukraine	2
			Belarus	2
	May	64	Romania	31
	June	65	Serbia	1
			Montenegro	1
			Albania	7
			Bosnia	3
			Herzegovina	2
	October	66	Poland	14
			Czech Republic	12
			Slovakia	9
			Hungary	28
			Romania	32
			Serbia	2

Year	Month	Mission	Destination	Visit
2011	February	67	Hungary	29
	June	68	Poland	15
	July	69	Ethiopia	1
			Uganda	1
	October	70	Romania	33
			Hungary	30
			Herzegovina	3
			Serbia	3
2012	February	71	Romania	34
			Hungary	31
	May	72	Romania	35
			Hungary	32
	July/August	73	Poland	16
			Czech Republic	13
			Slovakia	10
	November	74	Macedonia	2
			Kosovo	1
			Albania	8
2013	February	75	Romania	36
			Hungary	33
	May	76	Romania	37
			Hungary	34
	August	77	Slovakia	11
	October	78	Slovakia	12
			Hungary	35
			Romania	38
			Serbia	4
			Herzegovina	4
2014	February	79	Serbia	5
			Hungary	36
	May	80	Romania	39
			Hungary	37
	July/August	81	Slovakia	13
	October	82	Macedonia	3
			Bulgaria	1
	November	83	Slovakia	14
			Hungary	38
			Romania	40
			Serbia	6
			Herzegovina	5

Year	Month	Mission	Destination	Visit
2015	January	84	Hungary	39
			Romania	41
			Serbia	7
	April	85	Egypt	1
	May	86	Romania	42
			Hungary	40
	August	87	Slovakia	15
	October	88	Slovakia	16
			Hungary	41
			Romania	43
			Serbia	8
			Herzegovina	6
	December	89	Slovakia	17
2016	February	90	Bulgaria	2
	June	91	Romania	44
	August	92	Slovakia	18
	September	93	Romania	45
	October	94	Romania	46
			Hungary	42
		95	Peru	1
2017	February	96	Belarus	3
	May/June	97	Romania	47
	August	98	Slovakia	19
	October	99	Portugal	1
	November	100	Hungary	43
			Serbia	9
			Macedonia	4
2018	March	101	Belarus	4
	May	102	Romania	48
	June/July	103	Egypt	2
	August	104	Romania	49
	September/October	105	Czech Republic	14
			Poland	17
			Slovakia	20
			Hungary	44
			Romania	50
			Serbia	10

Year	Month	Mission	Destination	Visit
2019	June	106	Togo	2
	August	107	Slovakia	21
			Hungary	45
			Romania	51
	September	108	Kenya	3
2020	March	109	Belarus	5
	July	110	Hungary	46
			Romania	52
2022	August	111	Slovakia	22
	September	112	Romania	53
	November	113	Albania	9
2023	February	114	Kenya	4
	March/April	115	Hungary	47
			Romania	54
	June	116	Rwanda	1
	September	117	Uganda	2
	November	118	Albania	10
			Macedonia	5
2024	June/July	119	Philippines	2
	August	120	Slovakia	23